MW01537853

Writing and coloring Fun                    @jadierillustrations

# Introduction

Writing and Coloring Fun, is a Beautiful Project aimed young Children, which seeks to make the learning process and development of motor skills a little more enjoyable, allowing them to have fun and encourage their creativity at the same time as they are learning.

In this Book you will find fully colorable illustrations, and, through the relationship of the images with the words and letters of the alphabet, it can make easier the process of fixation in the Child's memory.

This means that Writing and Coloring Fun will allow children to learn how trace letters, words and also have fun coloring while learning, all in the same Book.

We Believe that learning and fun shouldn't Be contrary concepts, which is why we hope you really enjoy this Book as much as we enjoy doing it

# This Book Belongs to:

AaBbCcDdEeFfGgHhIiJjKkLlMmNnOoPpQqRrSsTtUuVvWwXxYyZz

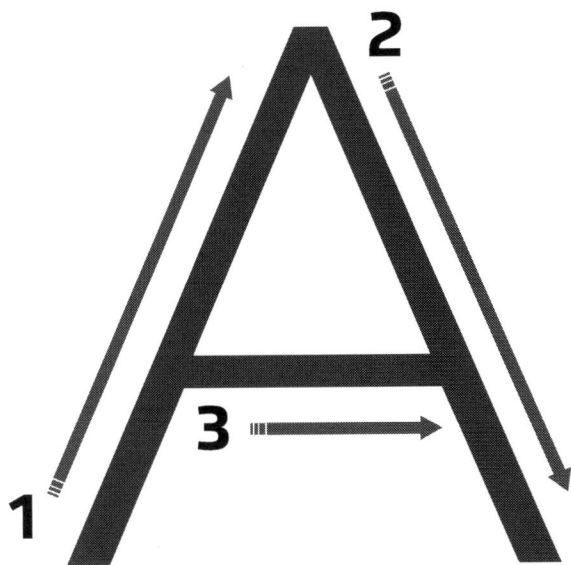

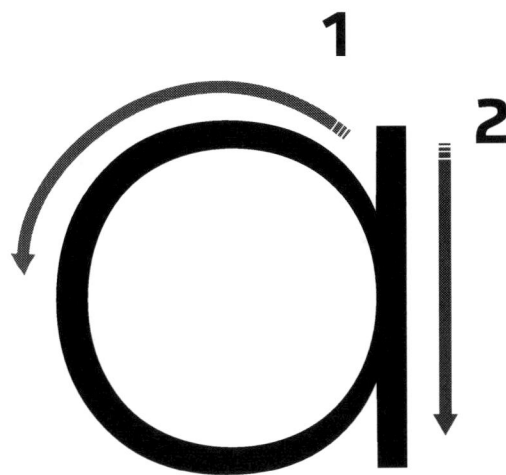

# A a

**2** **1**

**1** **3** **2**

# Airplane

A a

A a A A A A A A A

A A A A A A A A

a a a a a a a a a a a

a a a a a a a a a a

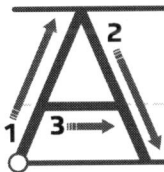

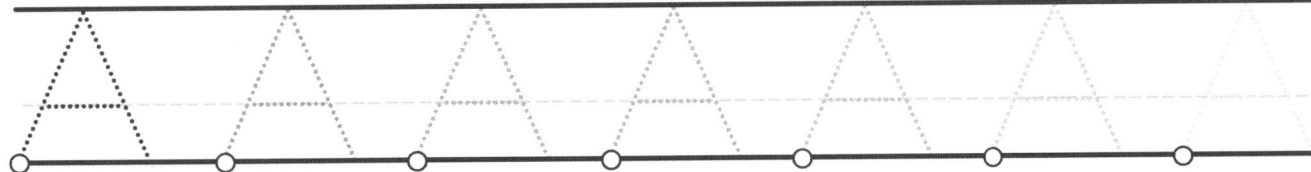

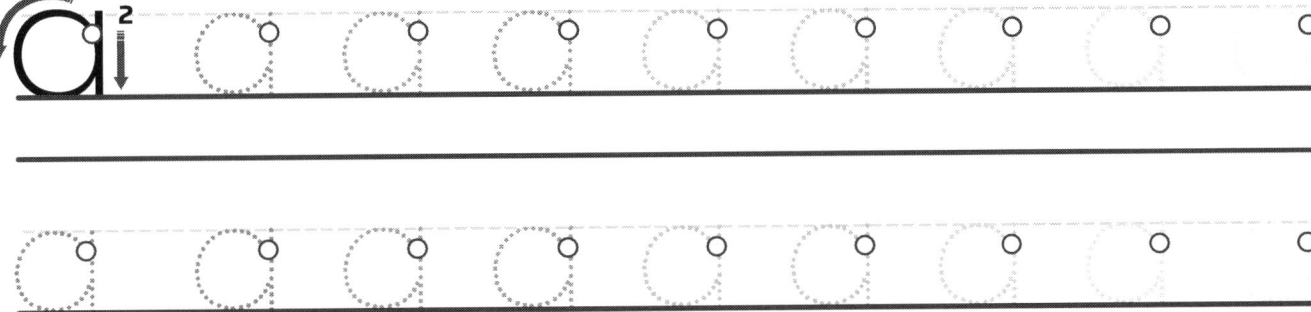

*Aa*BbCcDdEeFfGgHhIiJjKkLlMmNnOoPpQqRrSsTtUuVvWwXxYyZz

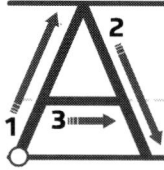

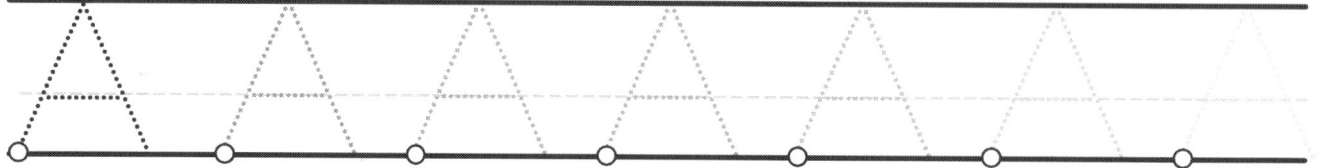

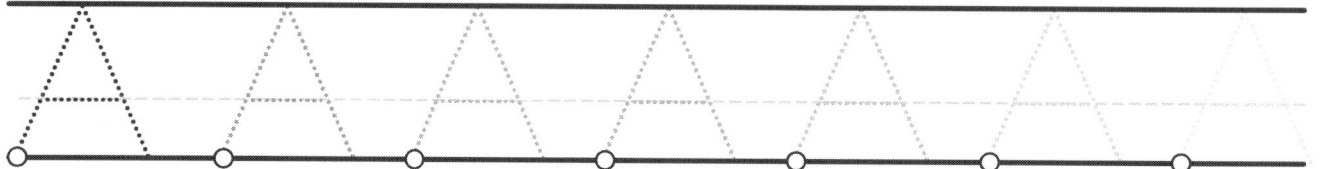

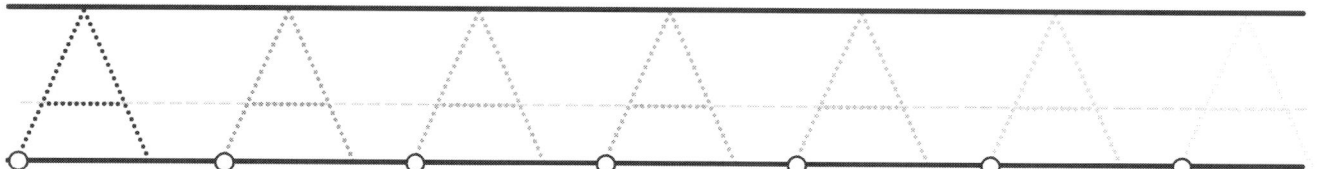

AaBbCcDdEeFfGgHhIiJjKkLlMmNnOoPpQqRrSsTtUuVvWwXxYyZz

# AIRPLANE

AIRPLANE

AIRPLANE

AIRPLANE

# airplane   airplane

airplane   airplane

airplane   airplane

airplane   airplane

*Aa*BbCcDdEeFfGgHhIiJjKkLlMmNnOoPpQqRrSsTtUuVvWwXxYyZz

AaBbCcDdEeFfGgHhIiJjKkLlMmNnOoPpQqRrSsTtUuVvWwXxYyZz

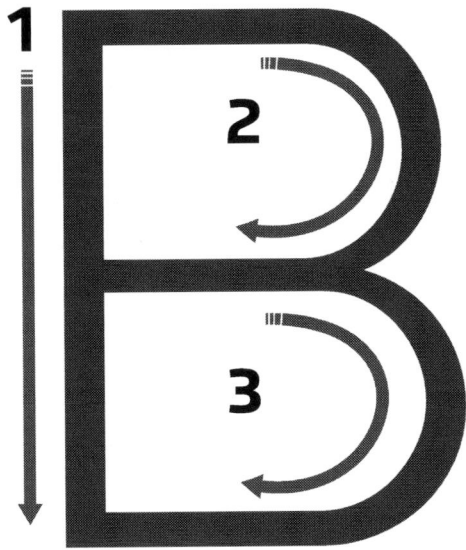
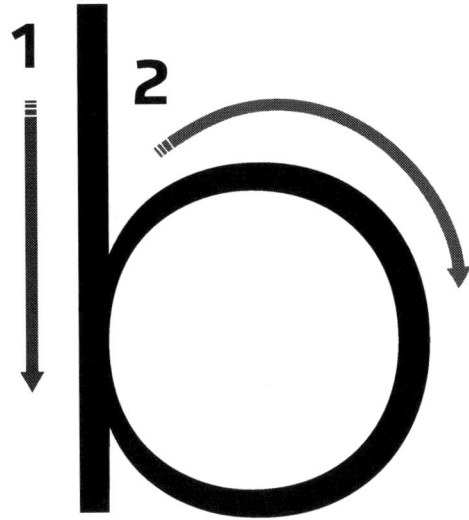

# Butterfly

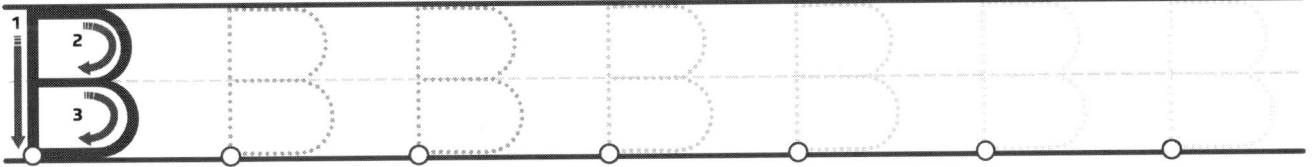

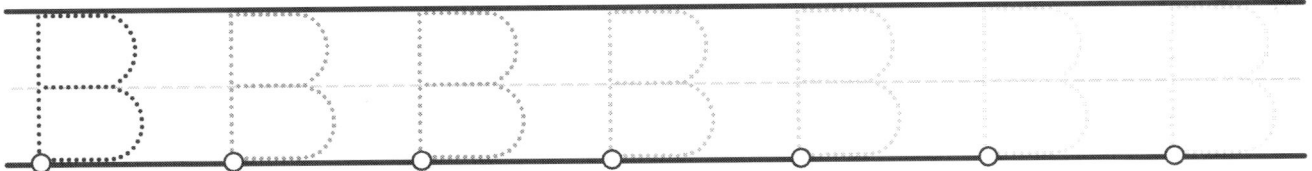

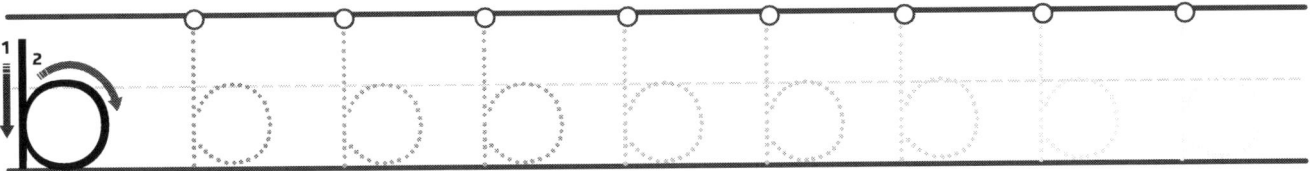

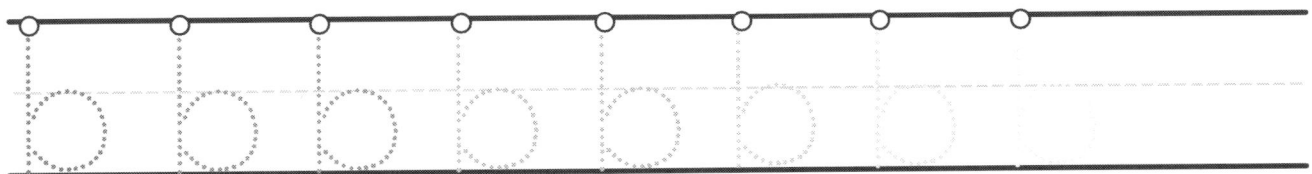

AbBbCcDdEeFfGgHhIiJjKkLlMmNnOoPpQqRrSsTtUuVvWwXxYyZz

B B B B B B B B

B B B B B B B B

B B B B B B B B

B B B B B B B B

b b b b b b b b

b b b b b b b b

b b b b b b b b

b b b b b b b b

# BUTTERFLY

BUTTERFLY

BUTTERFLY

BUTTERFLY

butterfly butterfly

butterfly butterfly

butterfly butterfly

butterfly butterfly

**AaBb**CcDdEeFfGgHhIiJjKkLlMmNnOoPpQqRrSsTtUuVvWwXxYyZz

AaBbCcDdEeFfGgHhIiJjKkLlMmNnOoPpQqRrSsTtUuVvWwXxYyZz

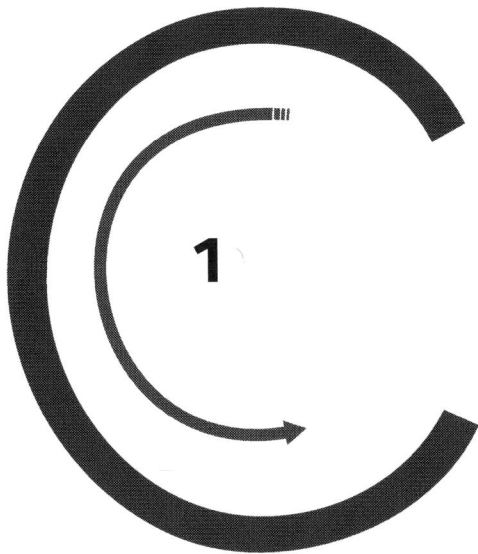

# C c

**Candy**

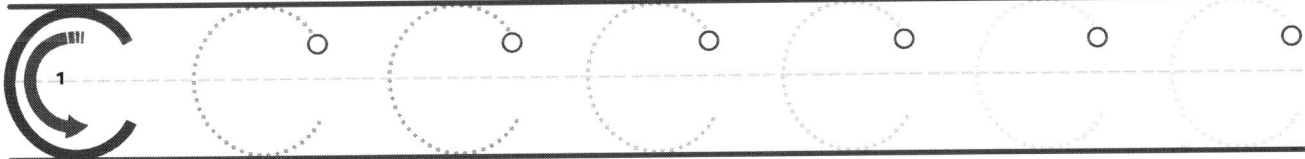

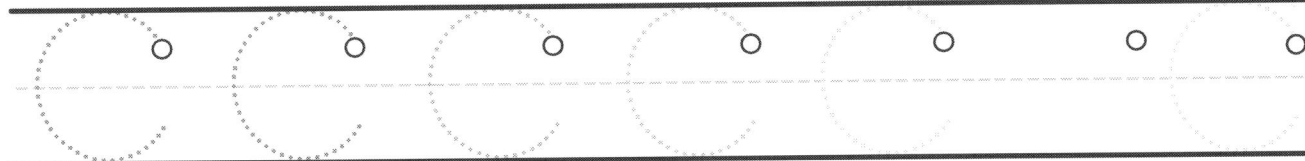

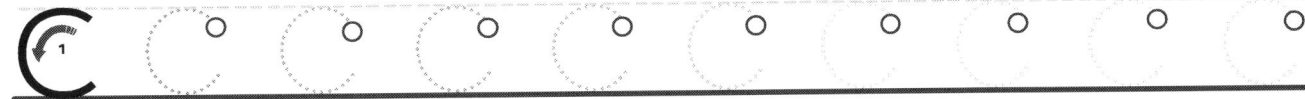

AaBb**Cc**DdEeFfGgHhIiJjKkLlMmNnOoPpQqRrSsTtUuVvWwXxYyZz

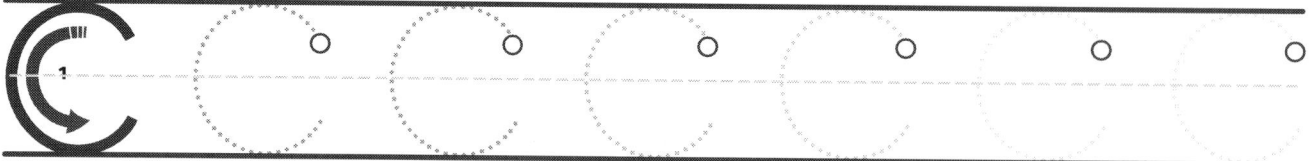

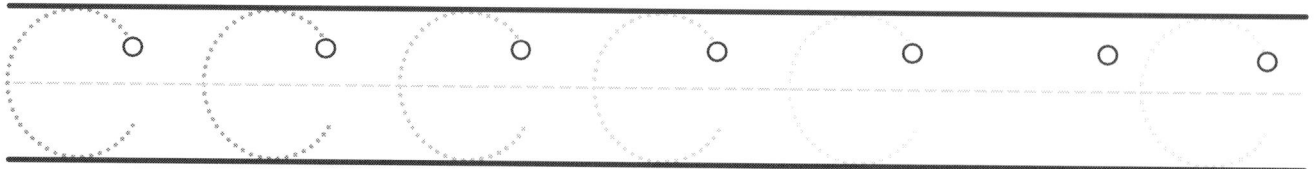

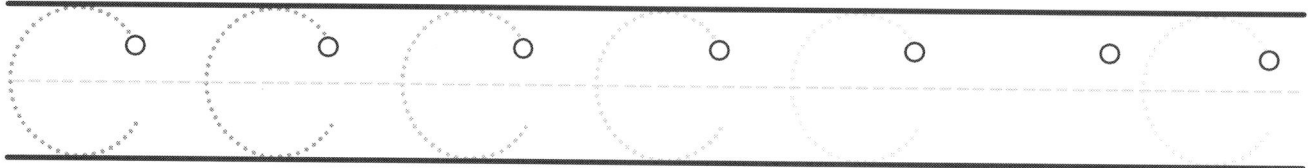

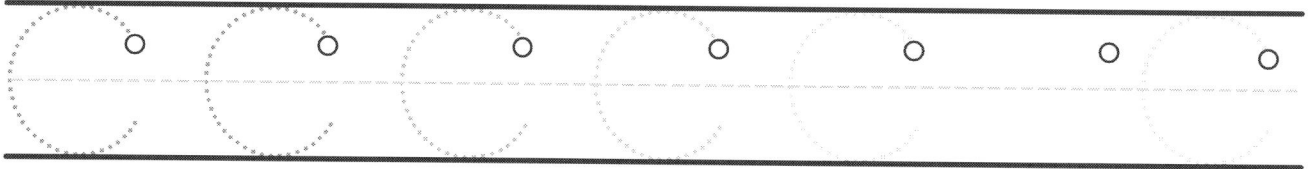

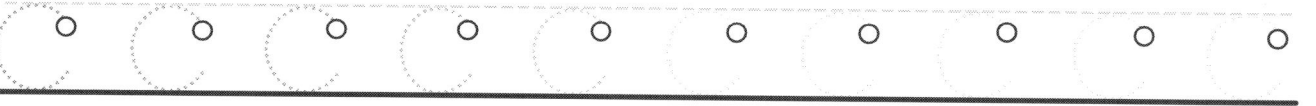

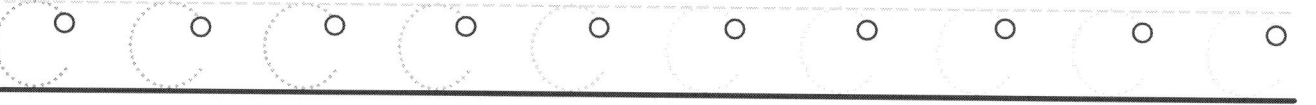

# CANDY

CANDY

CANDY

CANDY

candy   candy

candy   candy

candy   candy

candy   candy

*AaBbCcDdEeFfGgHhIiJjKkLlMmNnOoPpQqRrSsTtUuVvWwXxYyZz*

AaBbCcDdEeFfGgHhIiJjKkLlMmNnOoPpQqRrSsTtUuVvWwXxYyZz

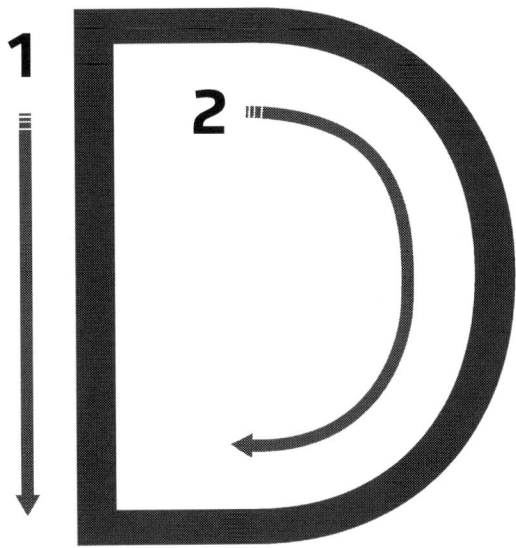

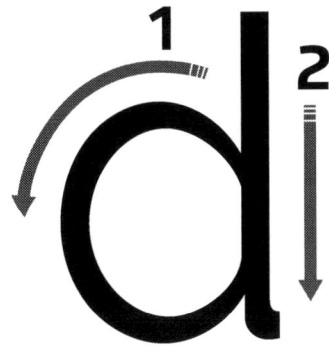

# Dolphin

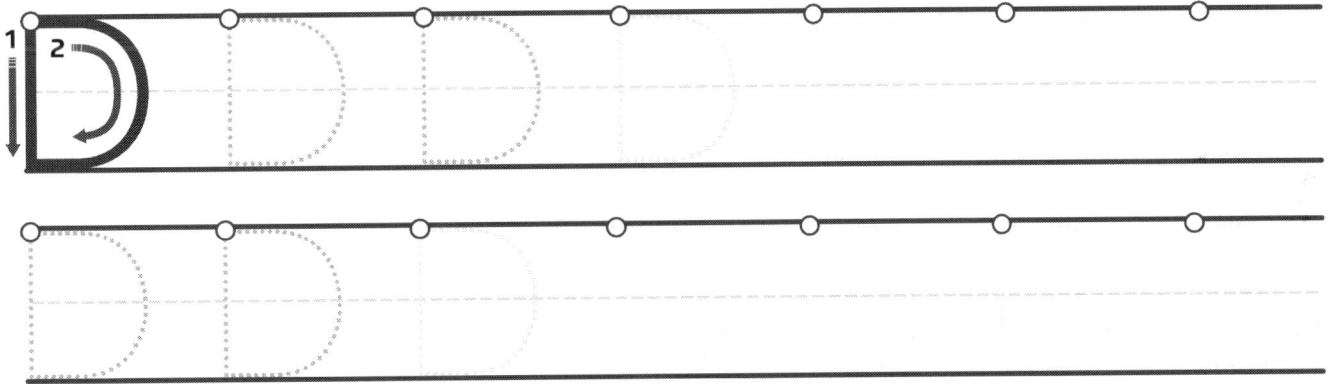

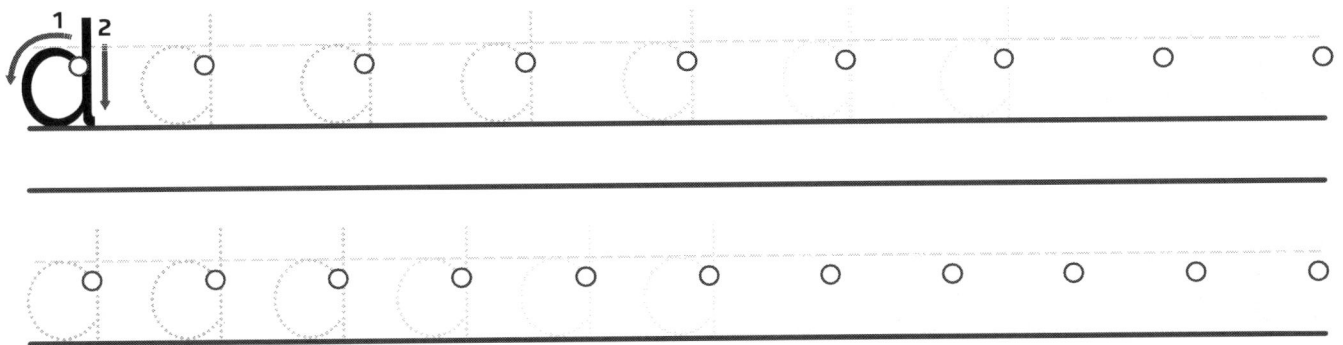

AaBbCc**Dd**EeFfGgHhIiJjKkLlMmNnOoPpQqRrSsTtUuVvWwXxYyZz

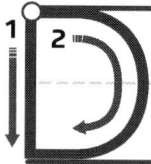

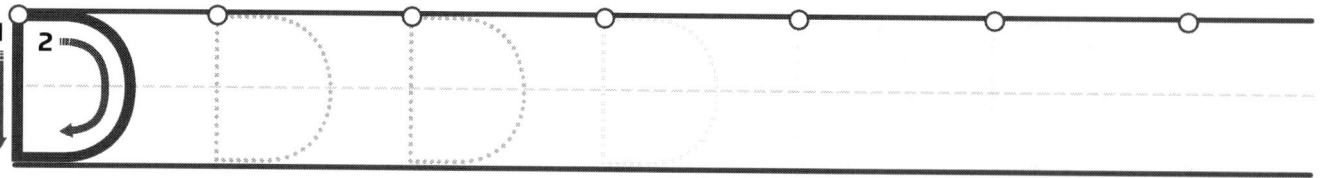

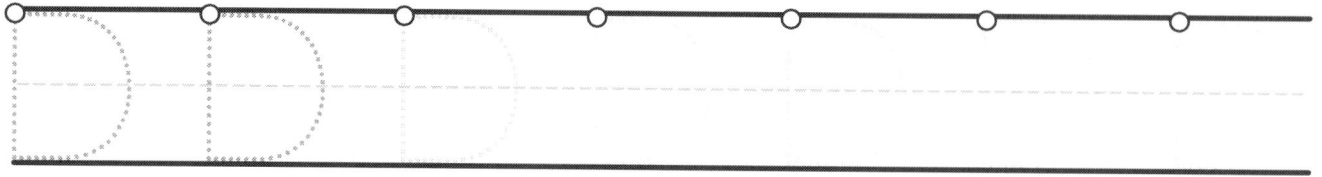

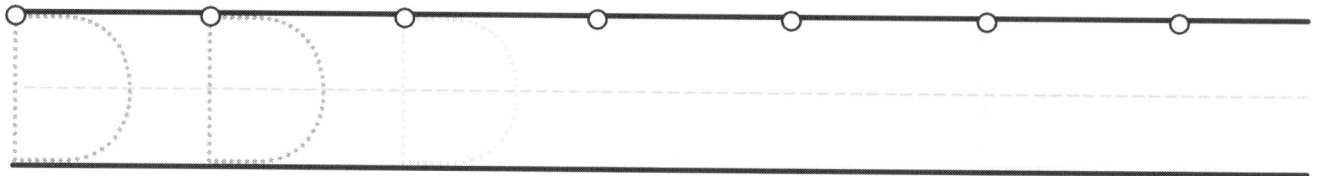

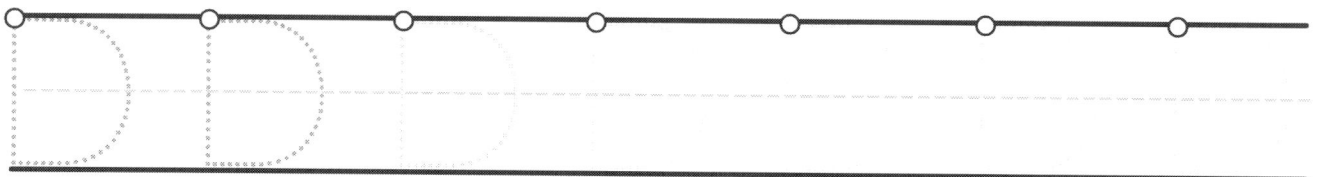

# DOLPHIN

DOLPHIN

DOLPHIN

DOLPHIN

**dolphin    dolphin**

dolphin    dolphin

dolphin    dolphin

dolphin    dolphin

AaBbCc**Dd**EeFfGgHhIiJjKkLlMmNnOoPpQqRrSsTtUuVvWwXxYyZz

AaBbCcDd**Ee**FfGgHhIiJjKkLlMmNnOoPpQqRrSsTtUuVvWwXxYyZz

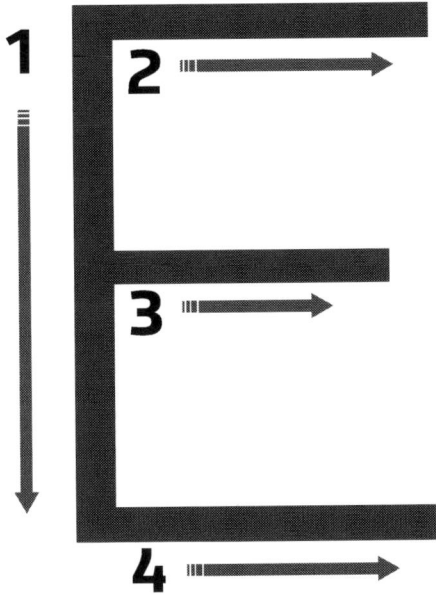

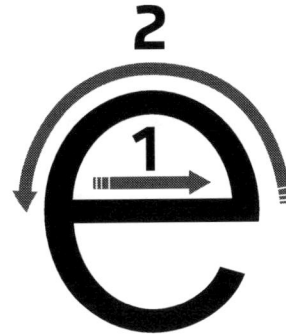

# Elephant

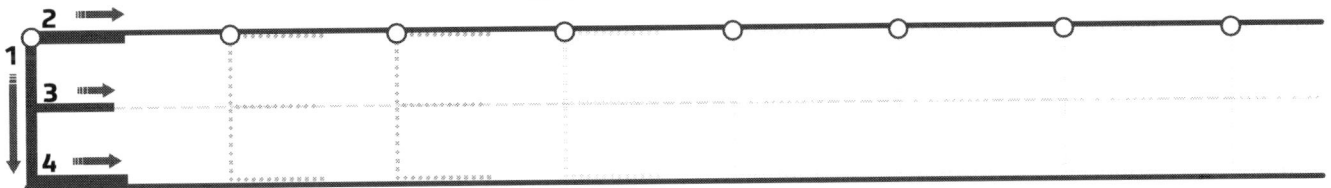

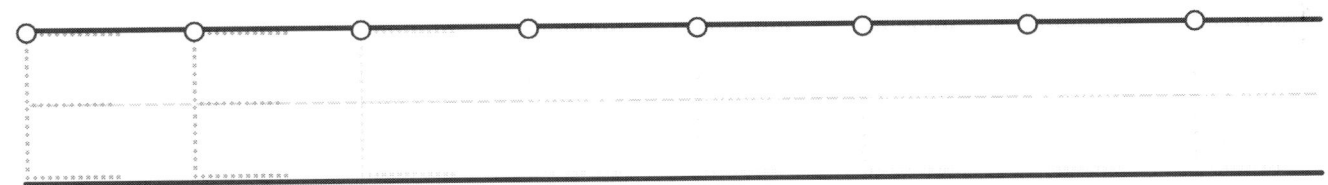

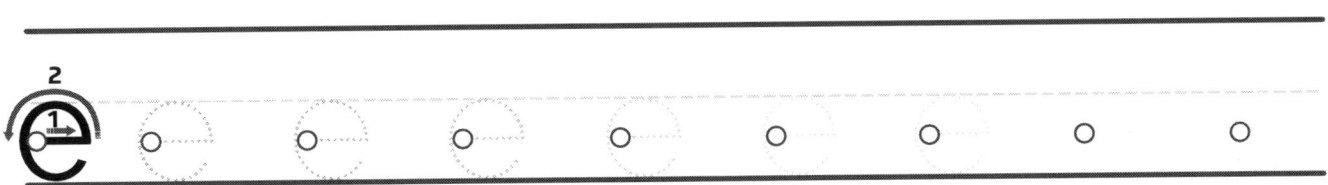

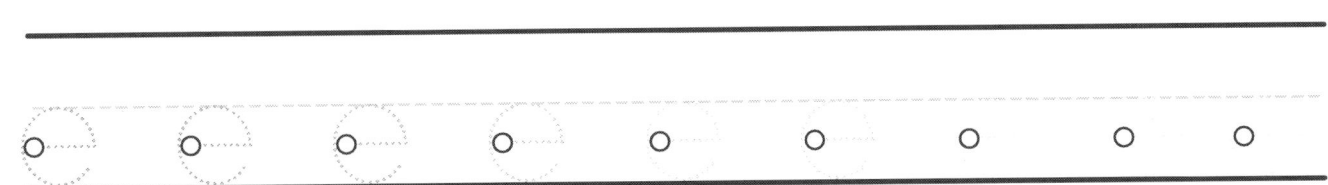

AaBbCcDd**Ee**FfGgHhIiJjKkLlMmNnOoPpQqRrSsTtUuVvWwXxYyZz

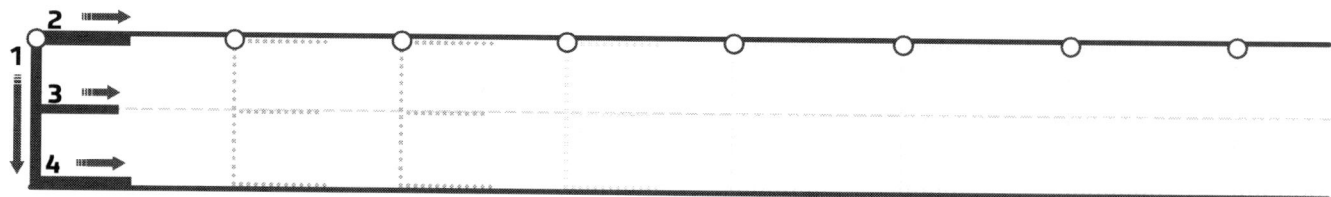

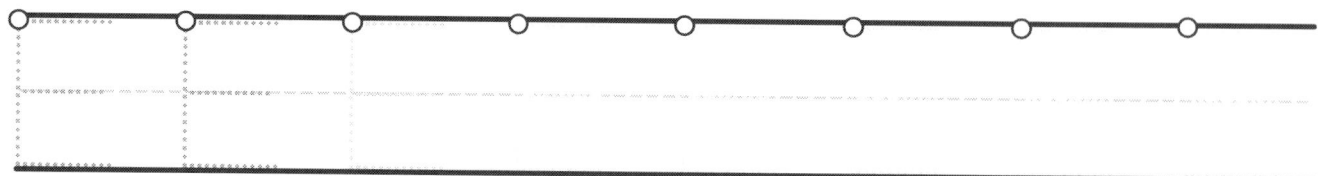

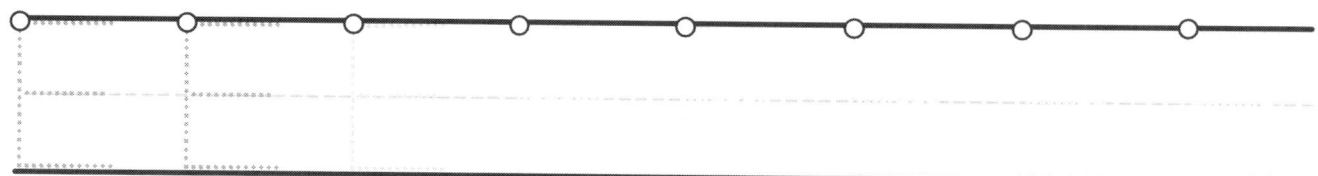

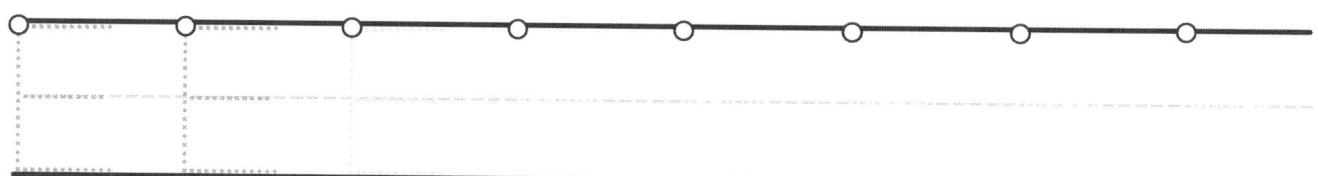

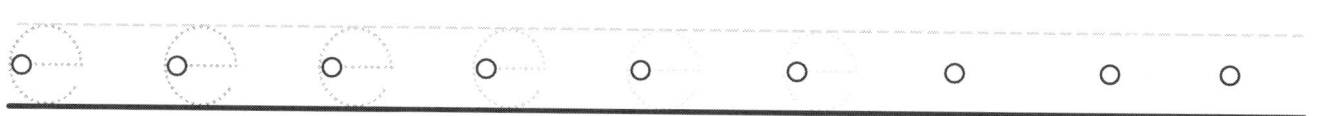

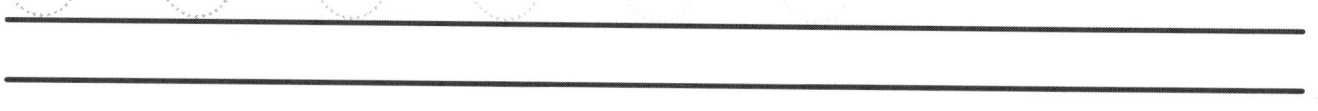

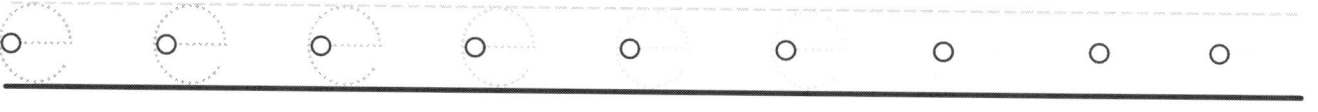

# ELEPHANT

ELEPHANT

ELEPHANT

ELEPHANT

## elephant

elephant

elephant

elephant

AaBbCcDd**Ee**FfGgHhIiJjKkLlMmNnOoPpQqRrSsTtUuVvWwXxYyZz

AaBbCcDdEe**Ff**GgHhIiJjKkLlMmNnOoPpQqRrSsTtUuVvWwXxYyZz

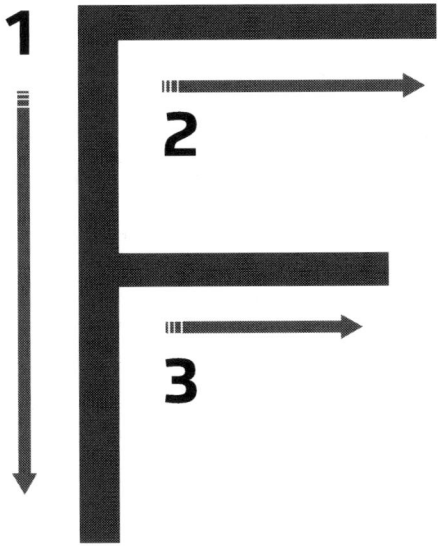

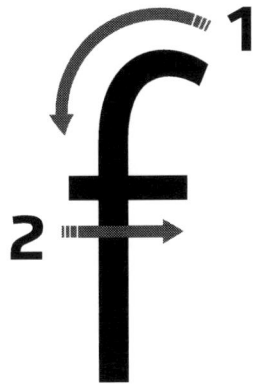

# Flower

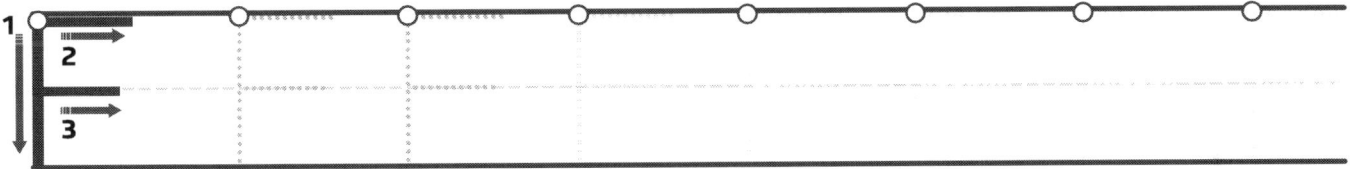

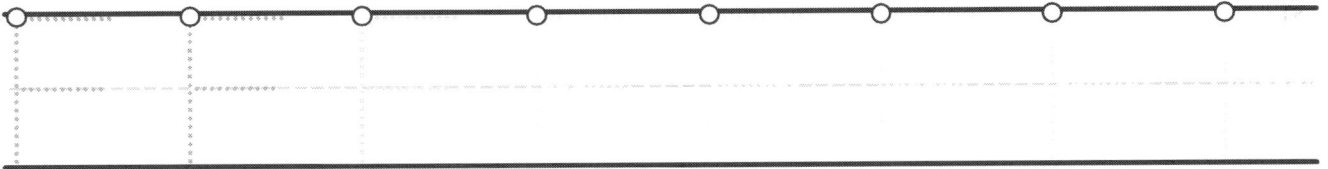

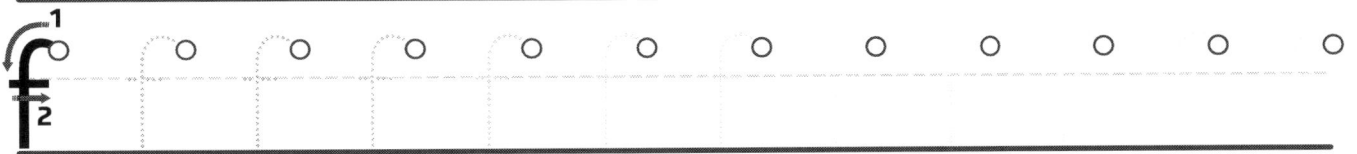

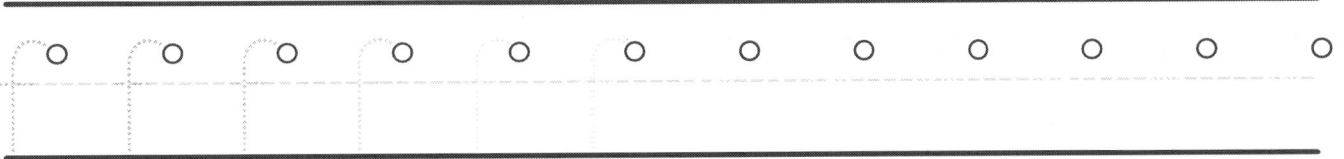

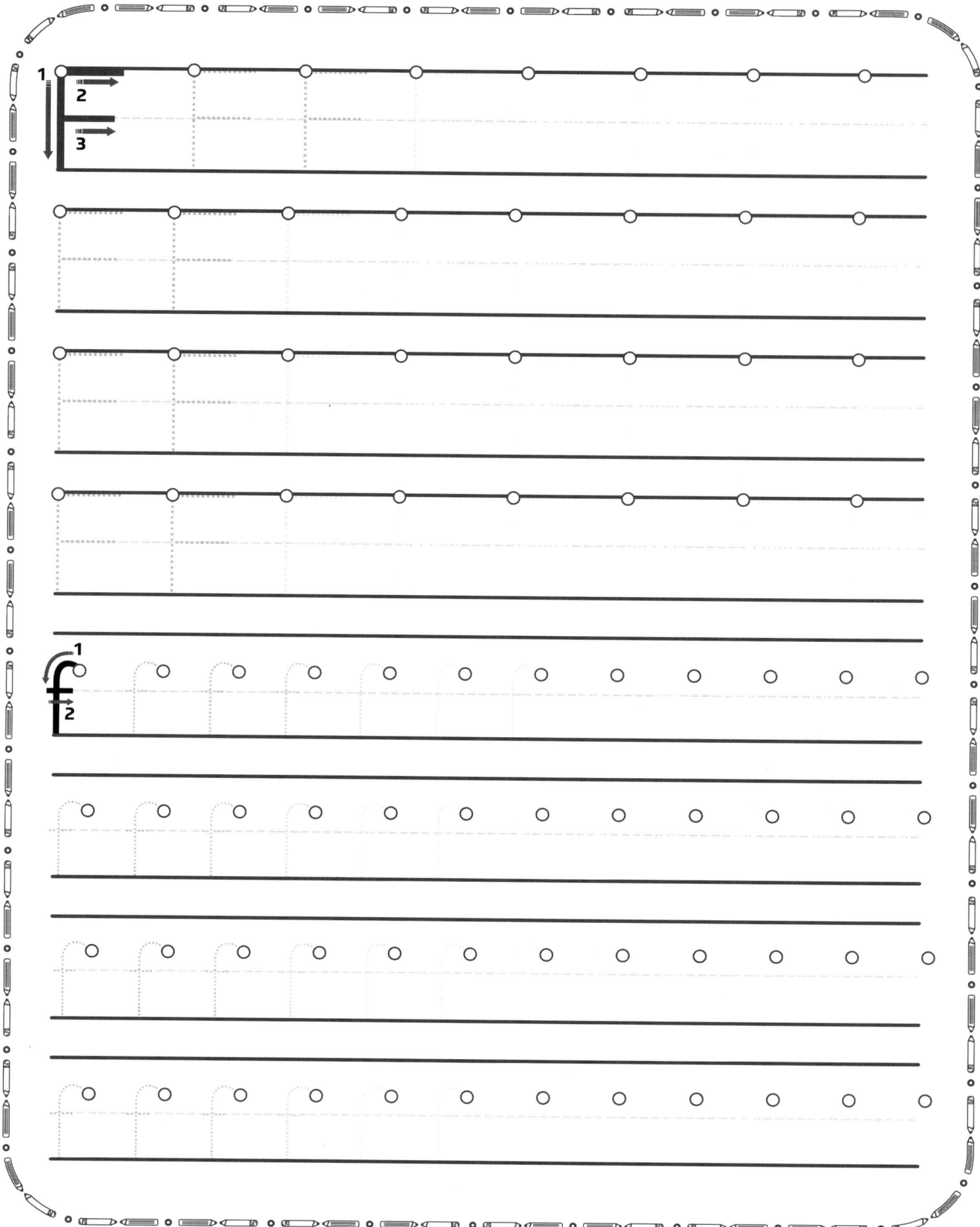

AaBbCcDdEe**Ff**GgHhIiJjKkLlMmNnOoPpQqRrSsTtUuVvWwXxYyZz

# FLOWER

FLOWER

FLOWER

FLOWER

flower     flower

flower     flower

flower     flower

flower     flower

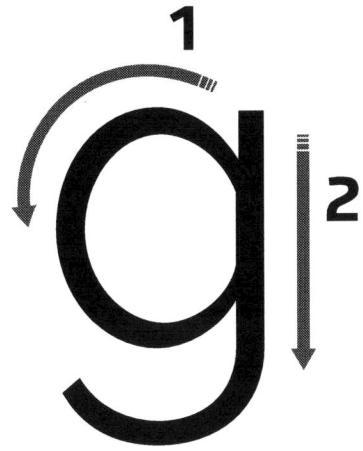

# Guitar

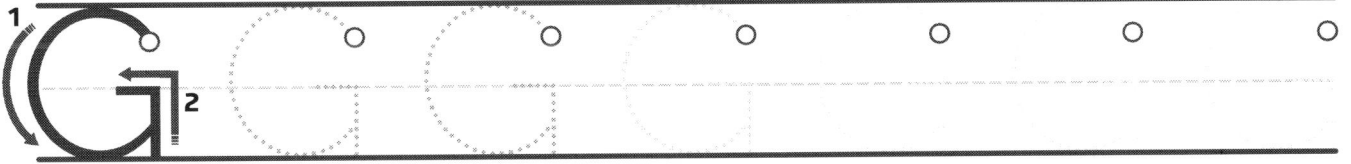
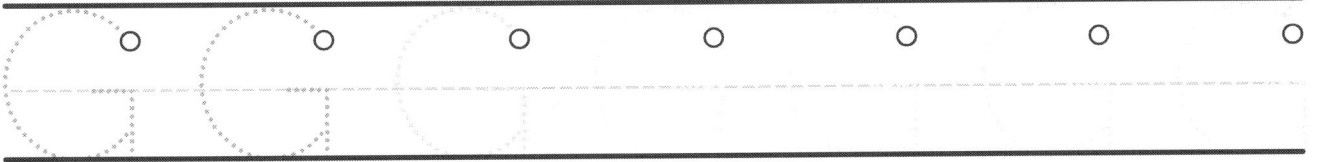
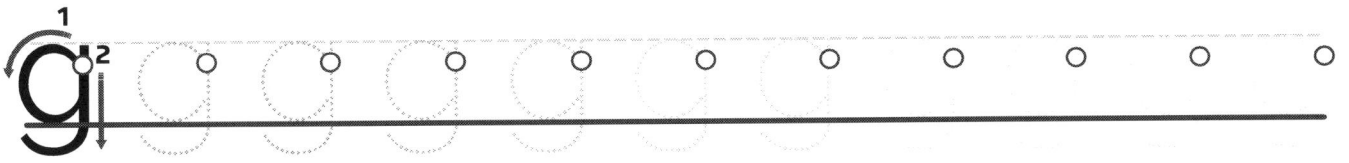
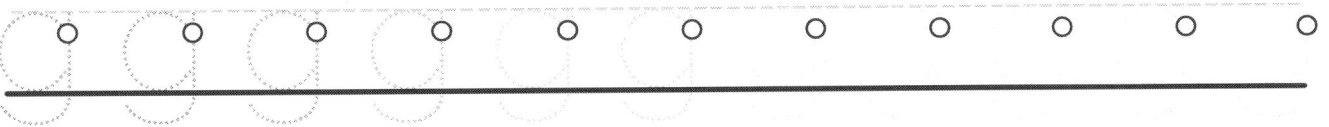

AaBbCcDdEeFf**Gg**HhIiJjKkLlMmNnOoPpQqRrSsTtUuVvWwXxYyZz

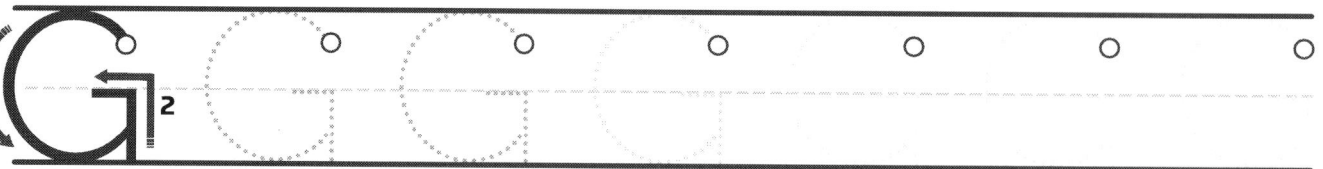

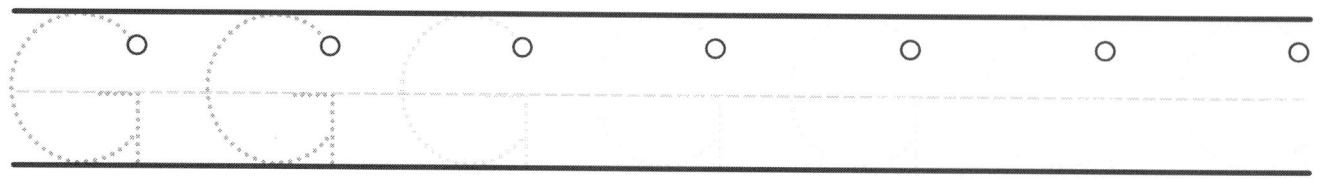

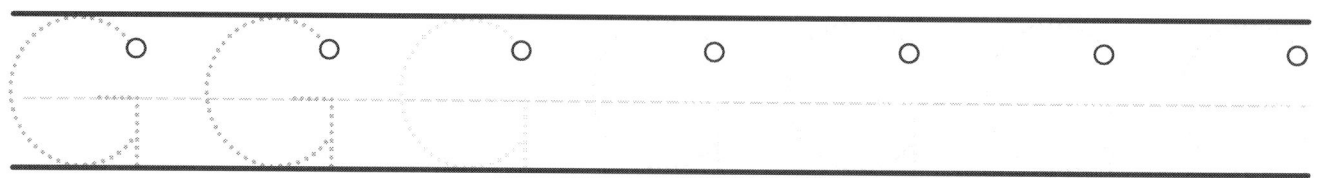

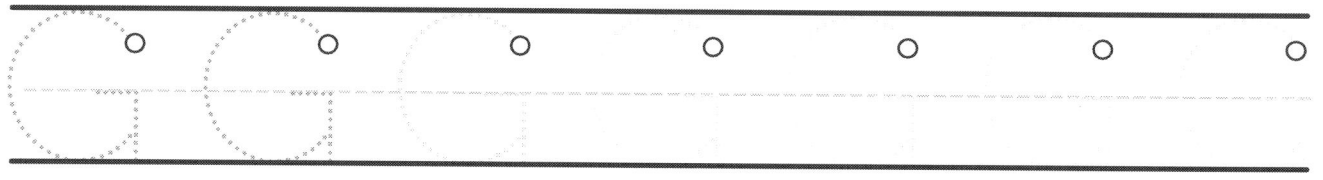

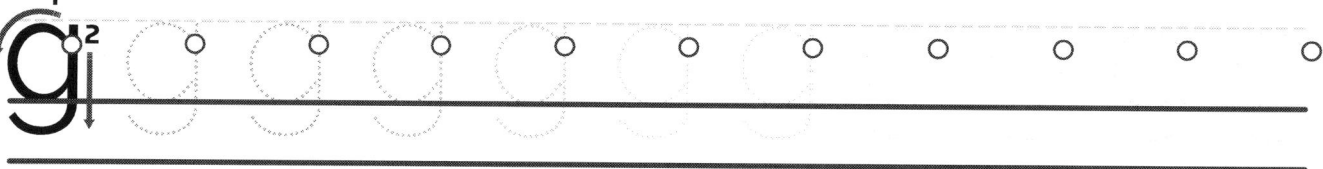

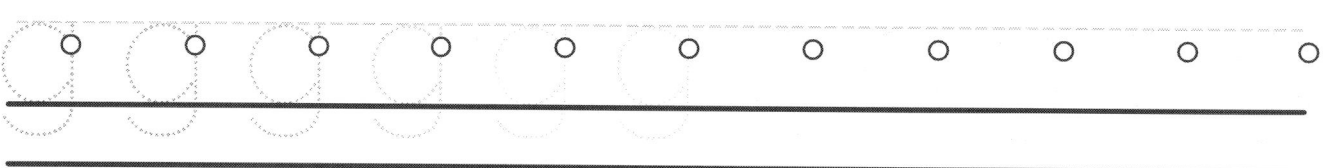

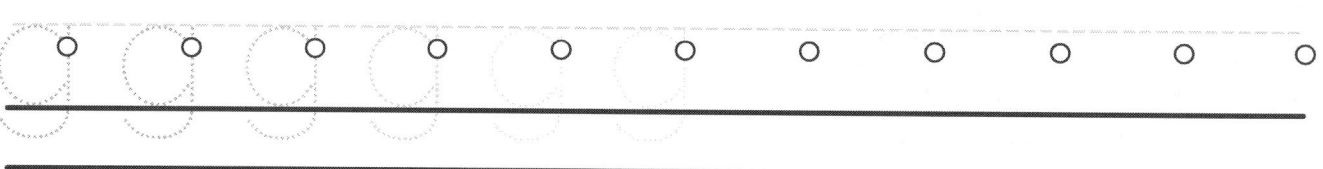

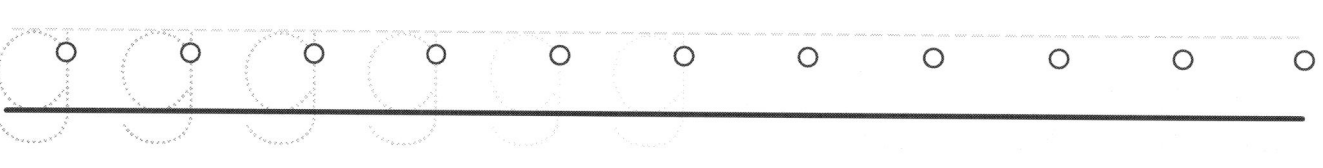

# GUITAR

GUITAR

GUITAR

GUITAR

guitar     guitar

guitar     guitar

guitar     guitar

guitar     guitar

AaBbCcDdEeFfGg**Hh**IiJjKkLlMmNnOoPpQqRrSsTtUuVvWwXxYyZz

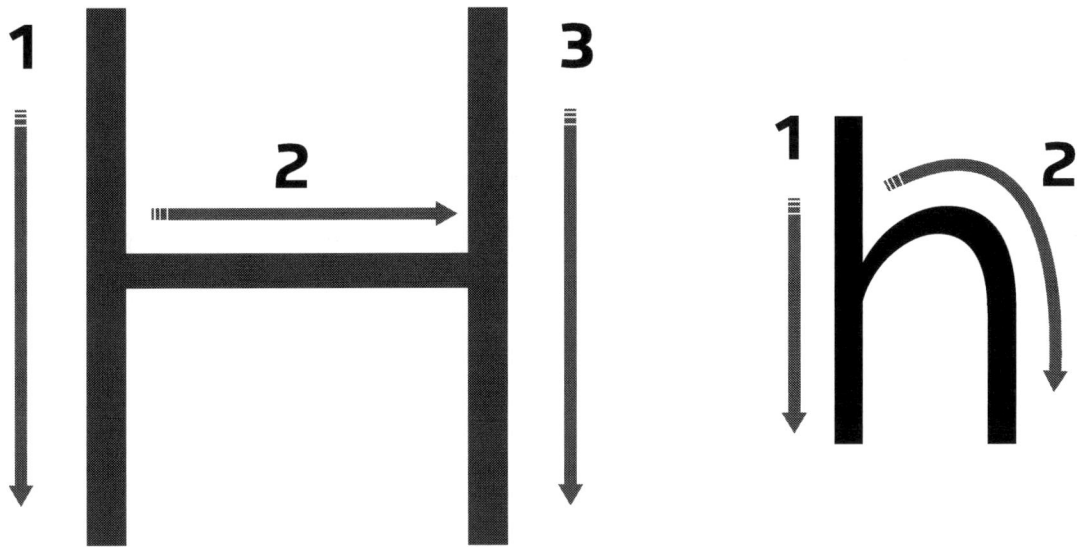

# Heart

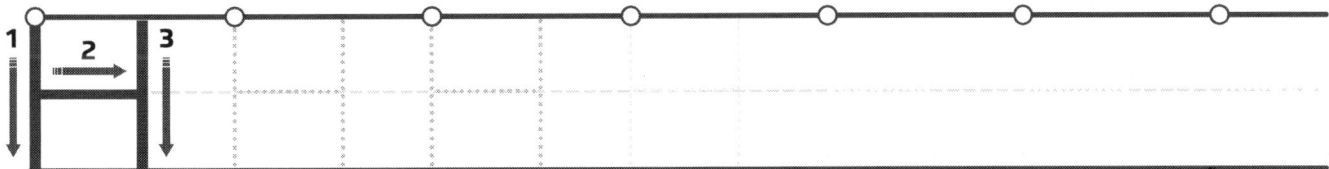

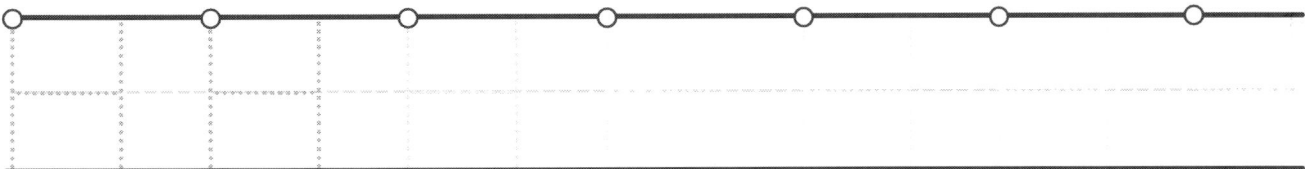

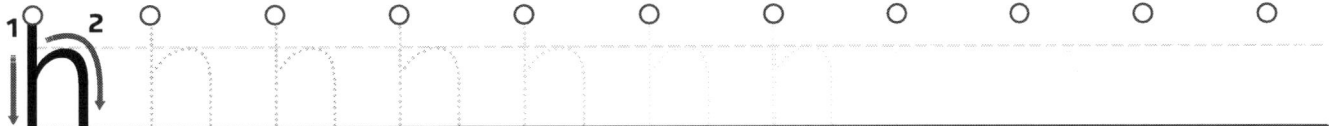

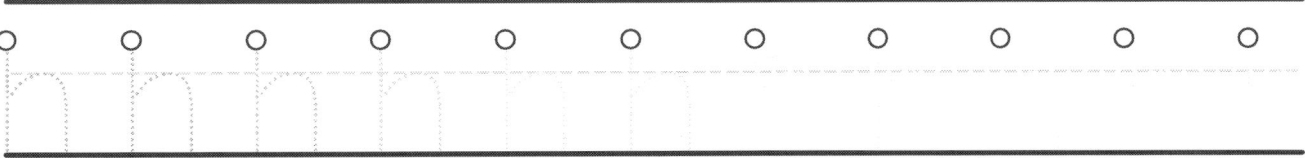

Hh

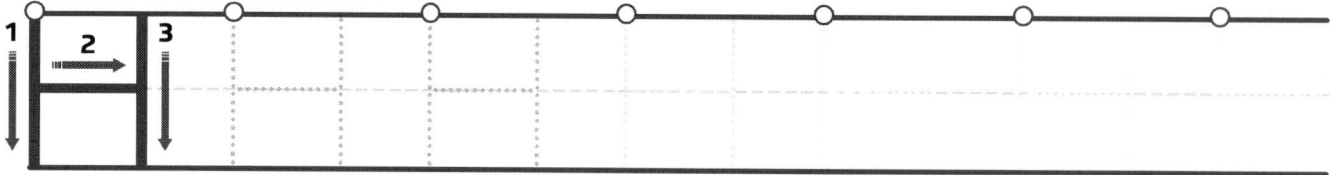

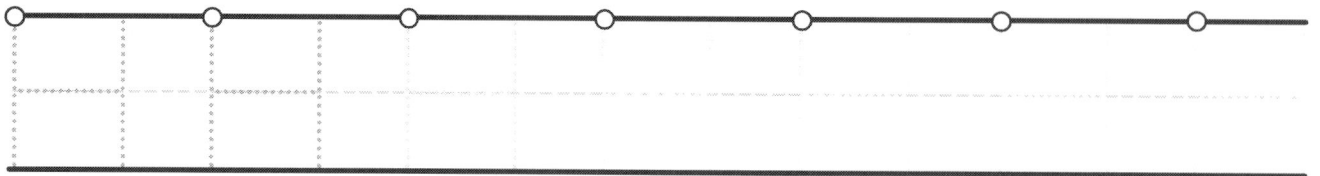

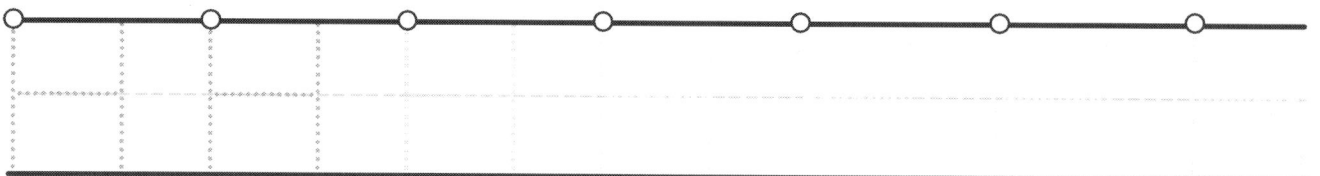

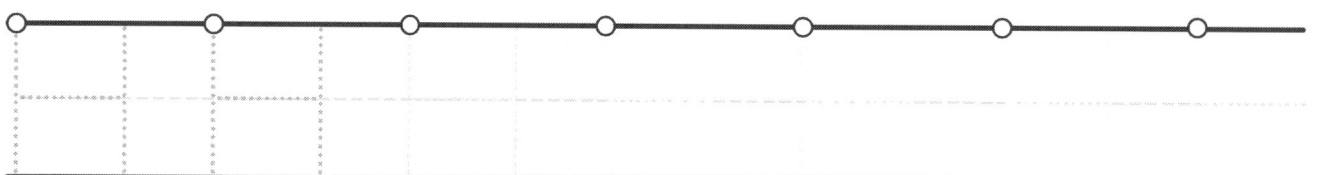

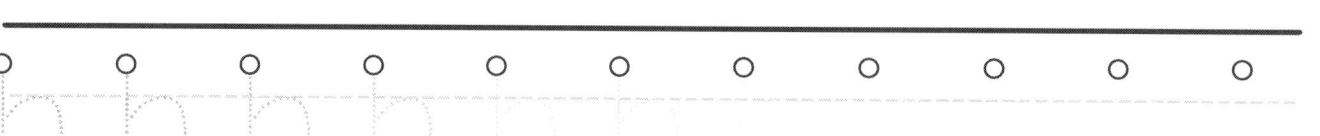

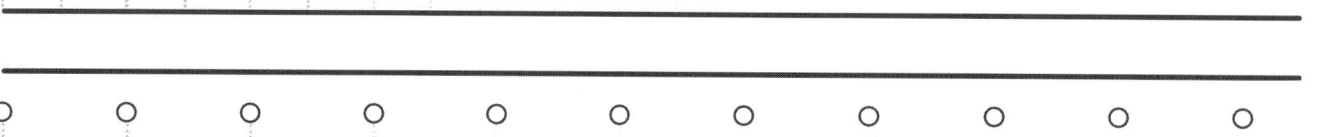

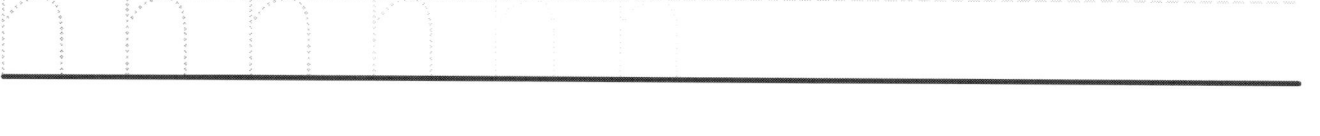

AaBbCcDdEeFfGg**Hh**IiJjKkLlMmNnOoPpQqRrSsTtUuVvWwXxYyZz

# HEART

HEART

HEART

HEART

heart heart heart

heart heart heart

heart heart heart

heart heart heart

AaBbCcDdEeFfGg**Hh**IiJjKkLlMmNnOoPpQqRrSsTtUuVvWwXxYyZz

AaBbCcDdEeFfGgHh**Ii**JjKkLlMmNnOoPpQqRrSsTtUuVvWwXxYyZz

**1**

**2**

**1**

# Island

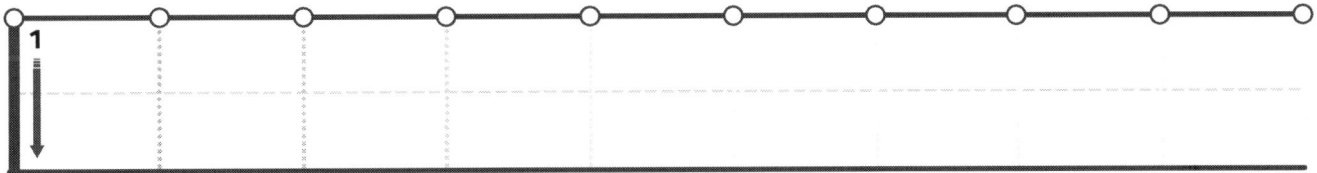

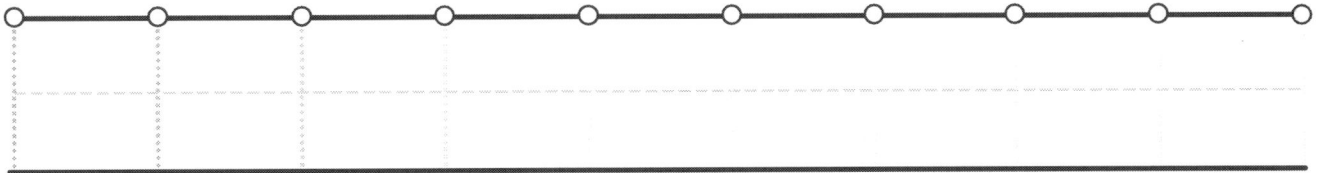

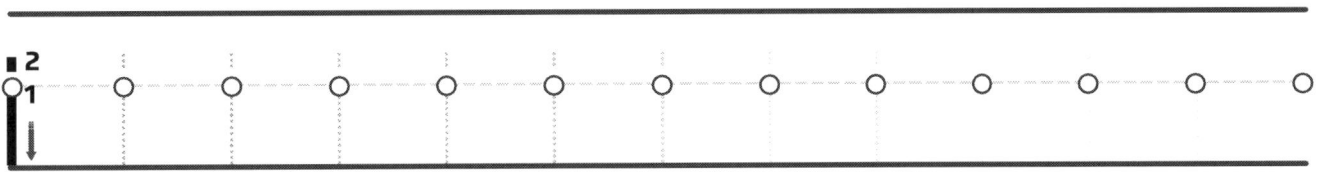

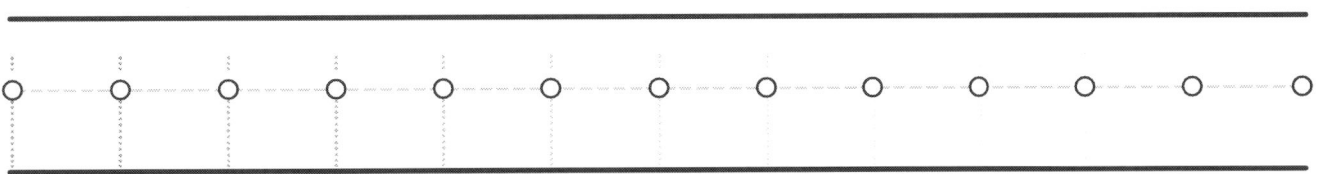

AaBbCcDdEeFfGgHh**Ii**JjKkLlMmNnOoPpQqRrSsTtUuVvWwXxYyZz

**1**

**2**
**1**

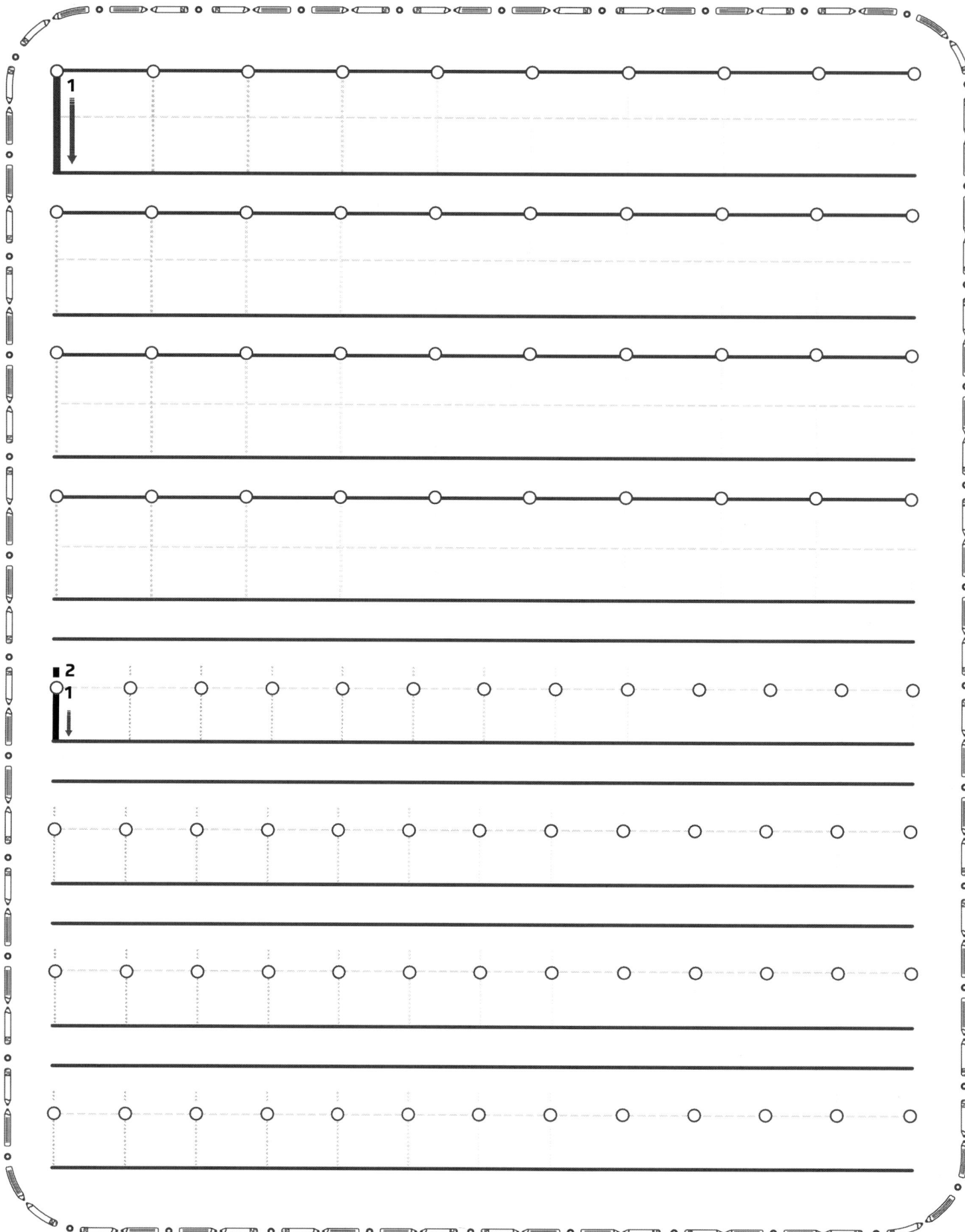

AaBbCcDdEeFfGgHh**Ii**JjKkLlMmNnOoPpQqRrSsTtUuVvWwXxYyZz

# ISLAND

ISLAND

ISLAND

ISLAND

island   island

island   island

island   island

island   island

*AaBbCcDdEeFfGgHh**Ii**JjKkLlMmNnOoPpQqRrSsTtUuVvWwXxYyZz*

AaBbCcDdEeFfGgHhIiJjKkLlMmNnOoPpQqRrSsTtUuVvWwXxYyZz

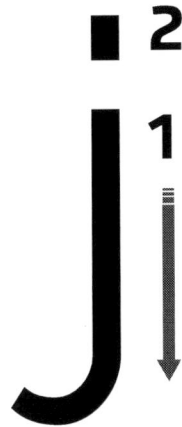

# Jam

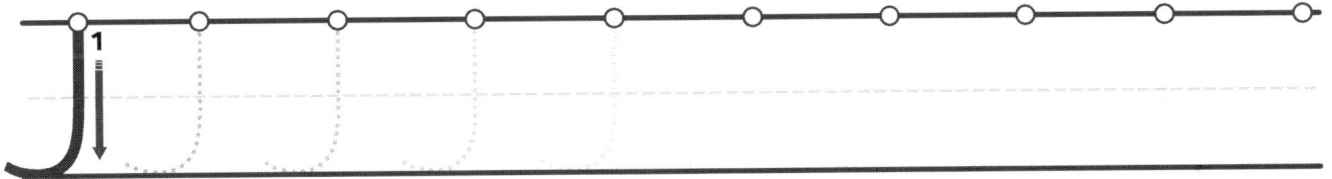
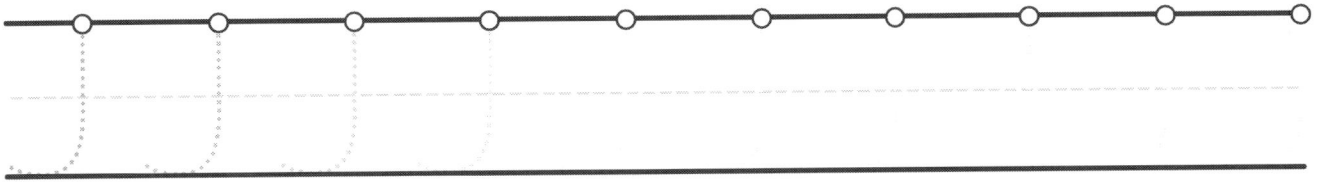
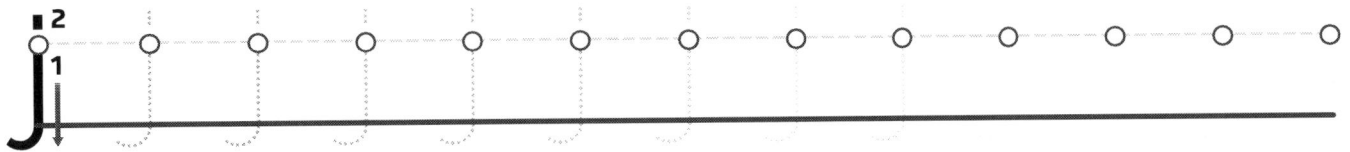
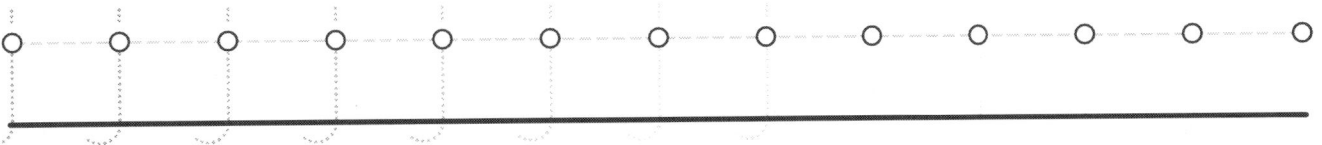

J

J j

AaBbCcDdEeFfGgHhIi**Jj**KkLlMmNnOoPpQqRrSsTtUuVvWwXxYyZz

# JAM JAM JAM

JAM JAM JAM JAM

JAM JAM JAM JAM

JAM JAM JAM JAM

# jam jam jam jam

jam jam jam jam

jam jam jam jam

jam jam jam jam

*AaBbCcDdEeFfGgHhIi**Jj**KkLlMmNnOoPpQqRrSsTtUuVvWwXxYyZz*

AaBbCcDdEeFfGgHhIiJj**Kk**LlMmNnOoPpQqRrSsTtUuVvWwXxYyZz

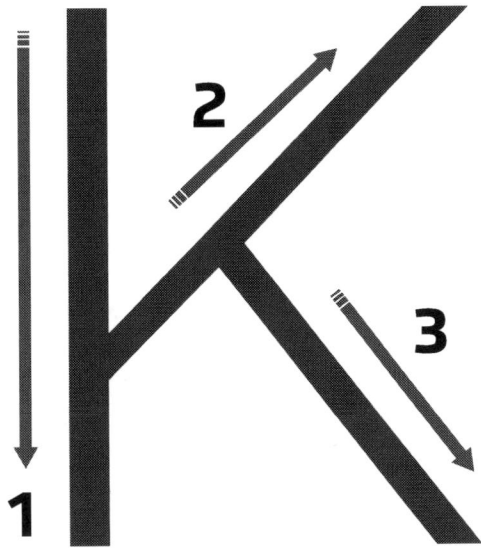
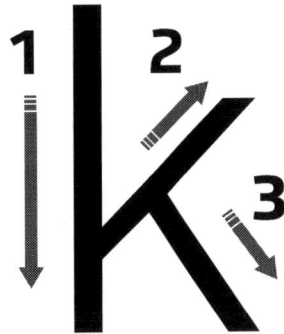

# Kitty

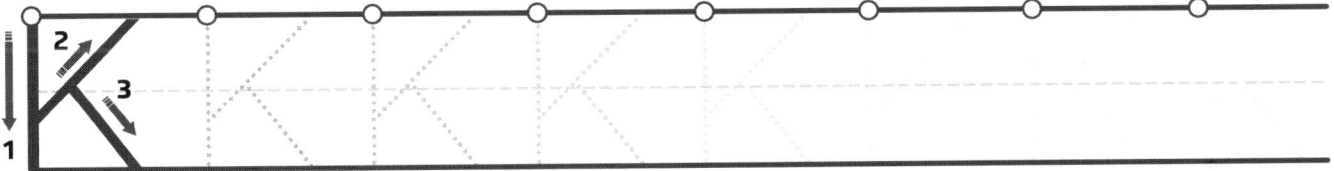

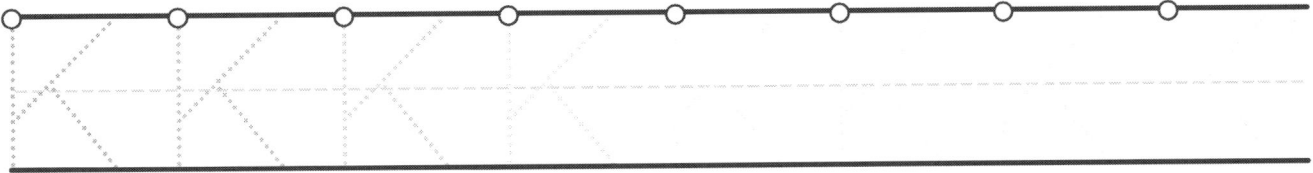

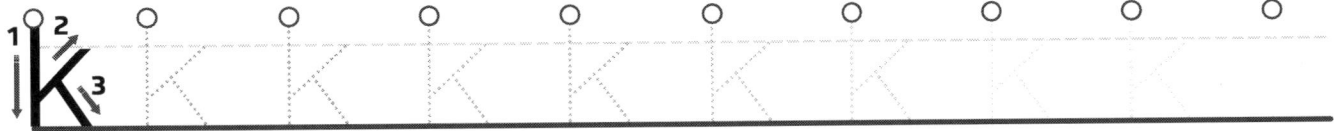

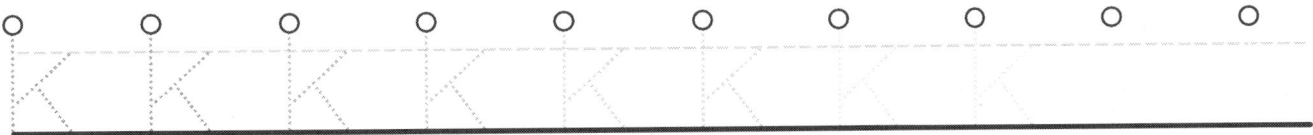

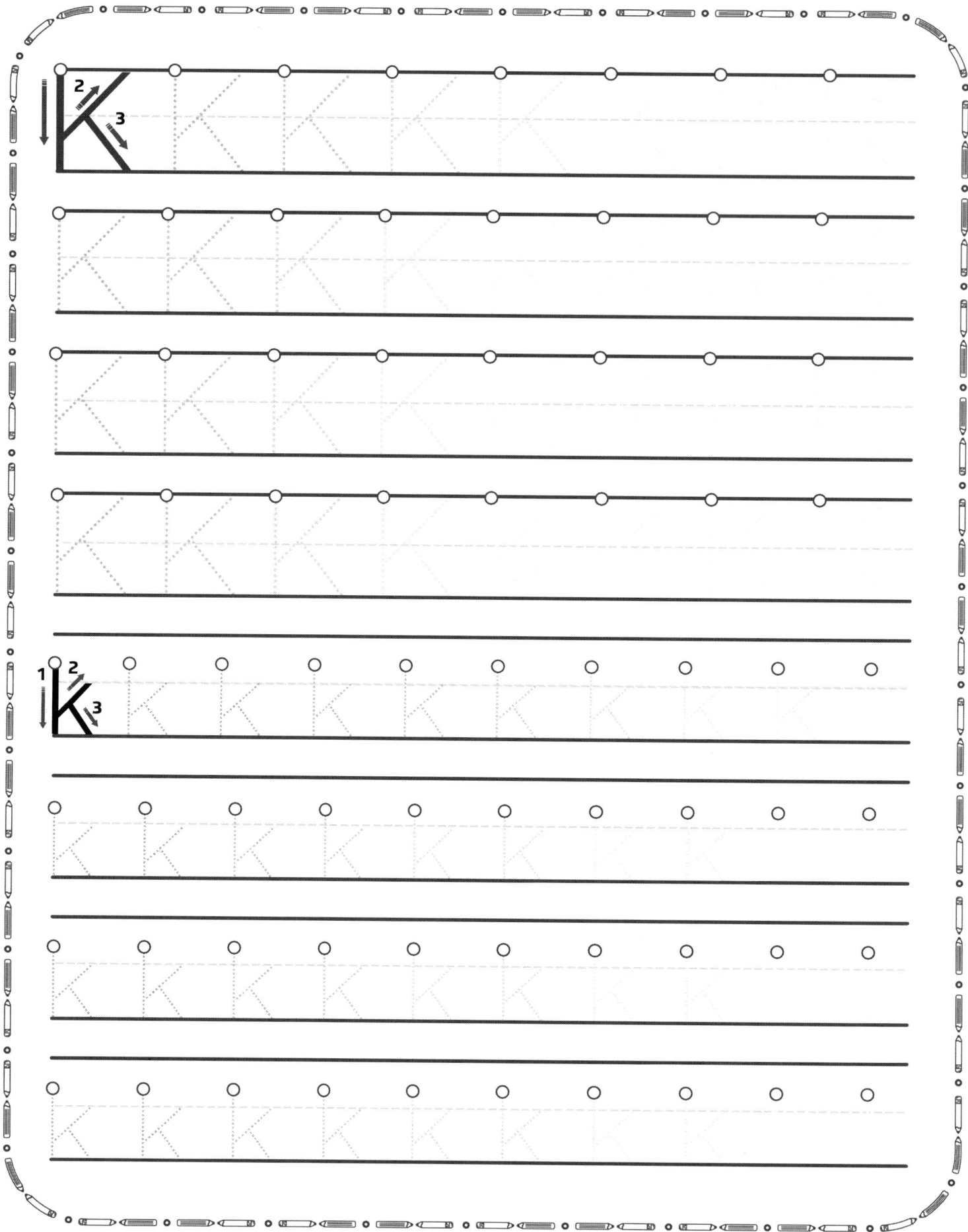

# KITTY KITTY

KITTY KITTY

KITTY KITTY

KITTY KITTY

## kitty    kitty    kitty

kitty    kitty    kitty

kitty    kitty    kitty

kitty    kitty    kitty

AaBbCcDdEeFfGgHhIiJj**Kk**LlMmNnOoPpQqRrSsTtUuVvWwXxYyZz

AaBbCcDdEeFfGgHhIiJjKkLlMmNnOoPpQqRrSsTtUuVvWwXxYyZz

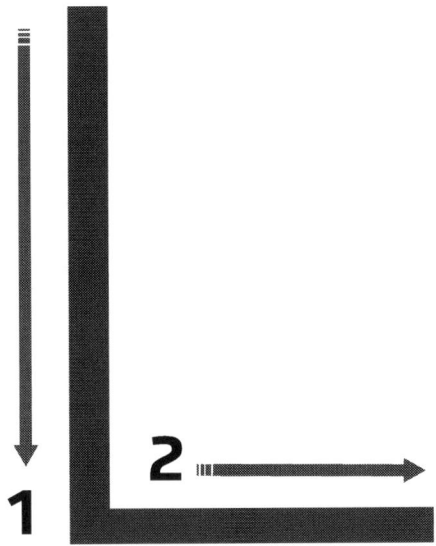

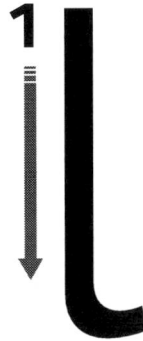

# Ladybug

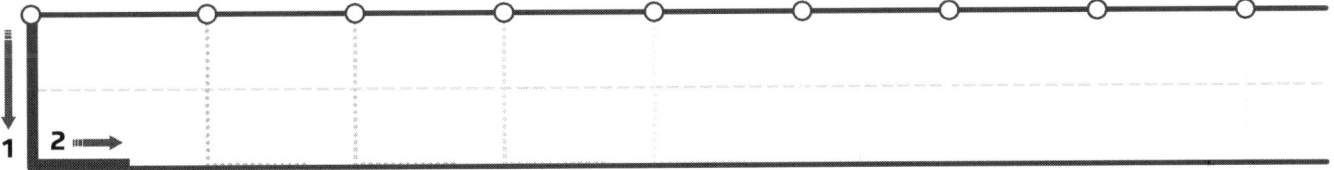

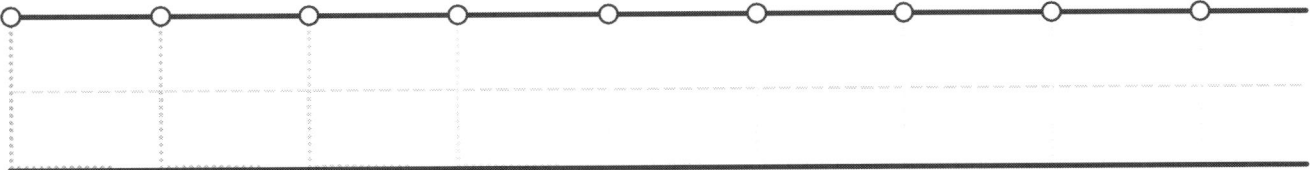

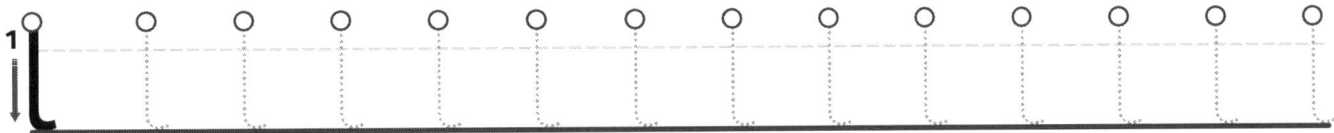

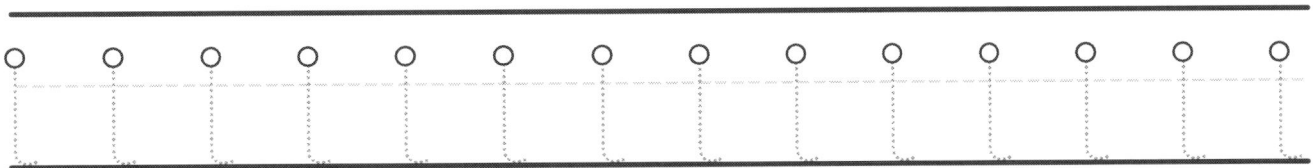

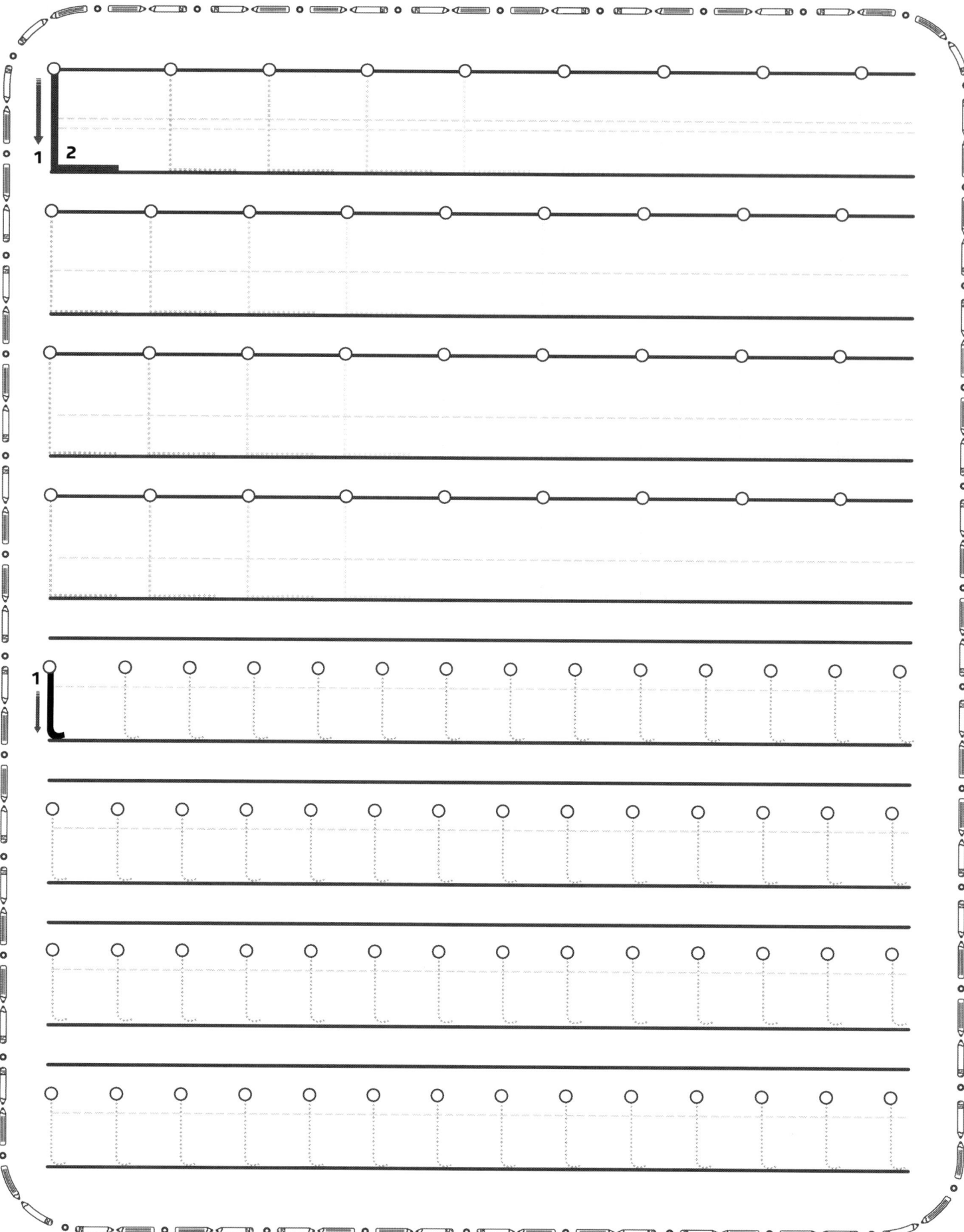

AaBbCcDdEeFfGgHhIiJjKk**Ll**MmNnOoPpQqRrSsTtUuVvWwXxYyZz

# LADYBUG

LADYBUG

LADYBUG

LADYBUG

# ladybug ladybug

ladybug ladybug

ladybug ladybug

ladybug ladybug

AaBbCcDdEeFfGgHhIiJjKk**Ll**MmNnOoPpQqRrSsTtUuVvWwXxYyZz

AaBbCcDdEeFfGgHhIiJjKkLl**Mm**NnOoPpQqRrSsTtUuVvWwXxYyZz

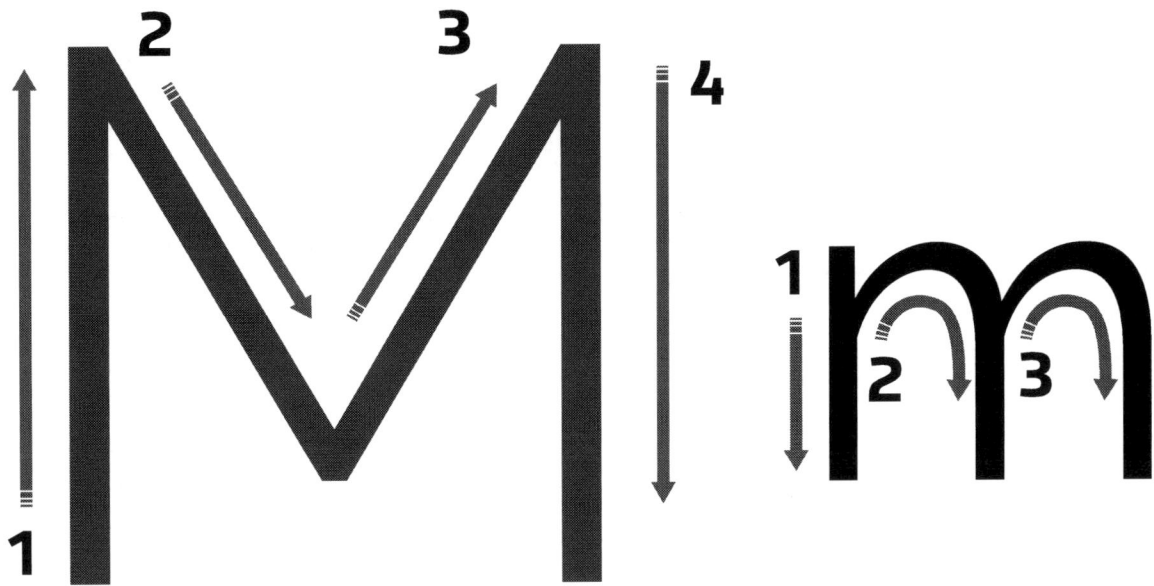

# Monkey

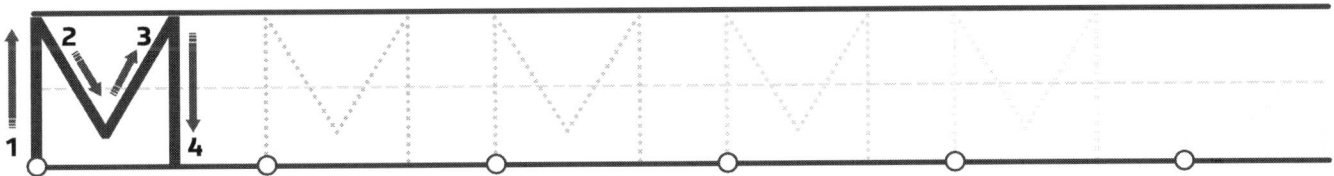

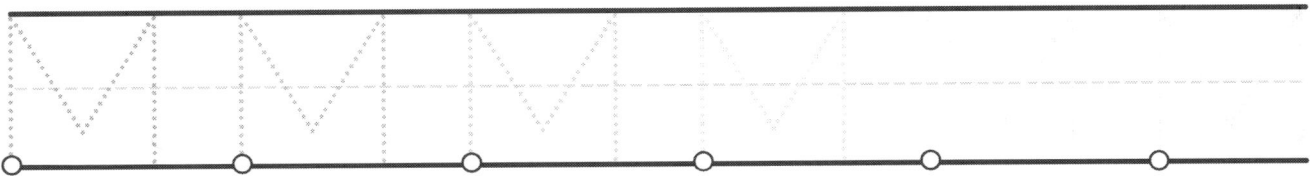

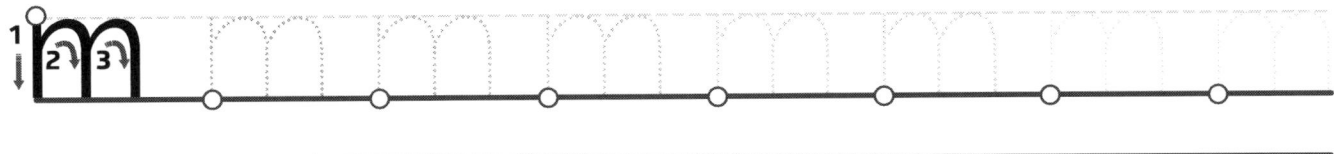

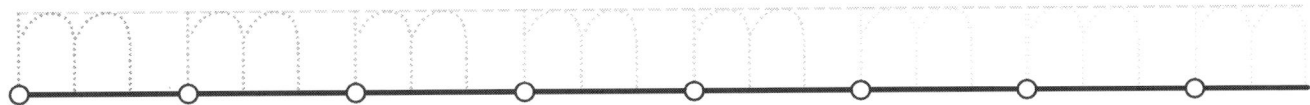

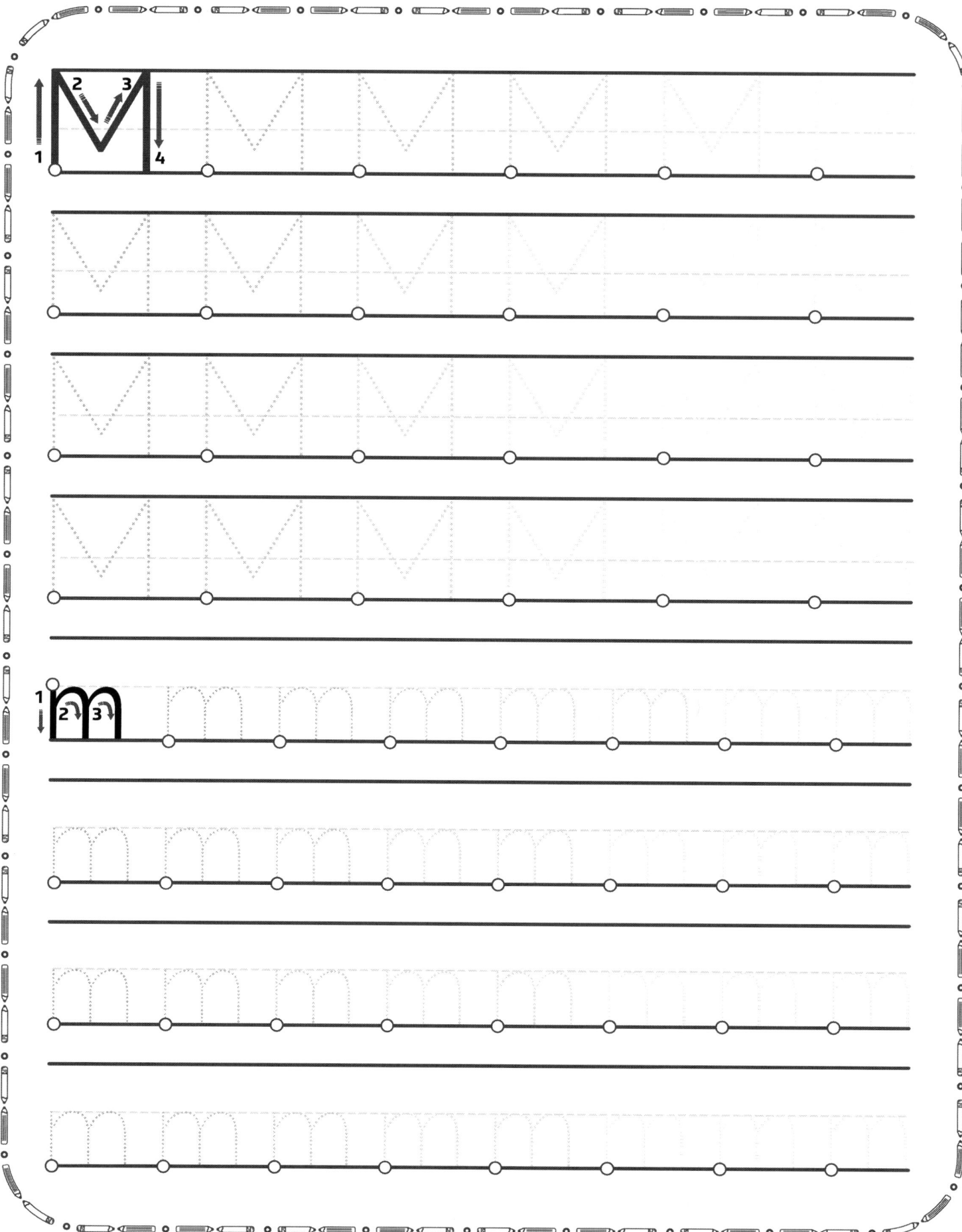

# MONKEY

MONKEY

MONKEY

MONKEY

## monkey monkey

monkey monkey

monkey monkey

monkey monkey

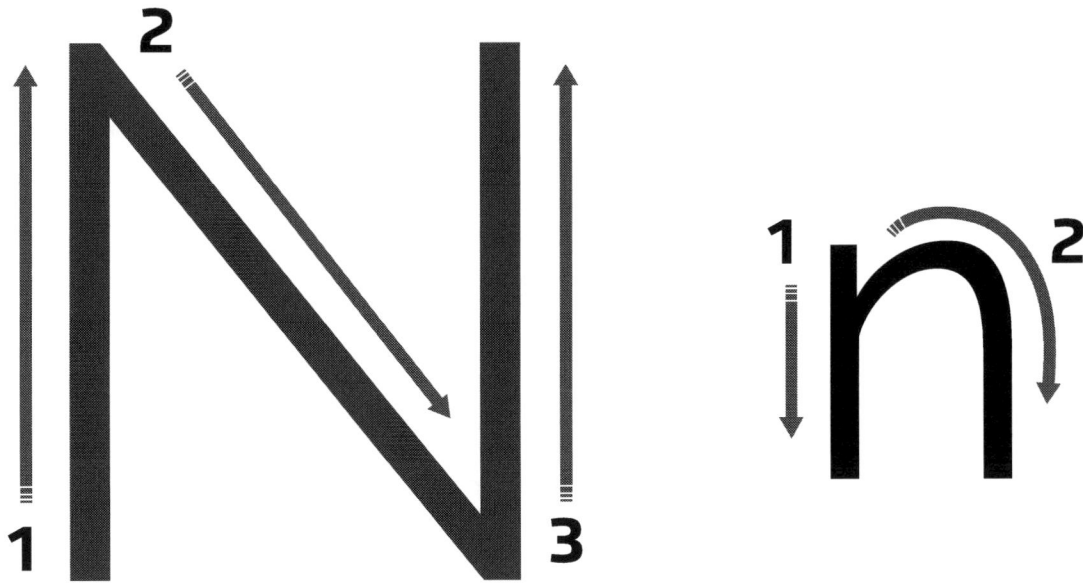

# Necklace

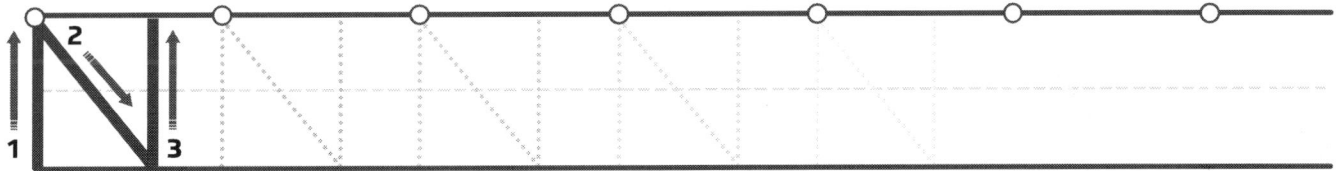

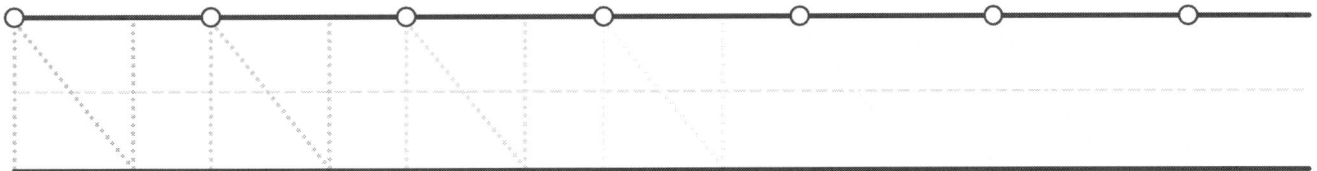

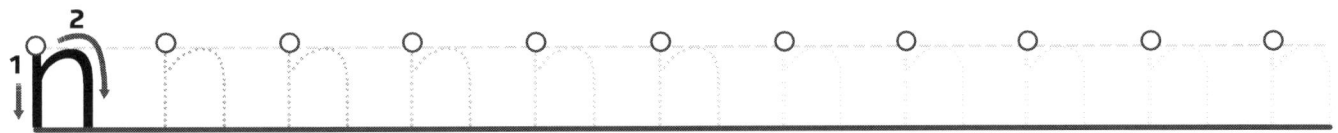

N

n

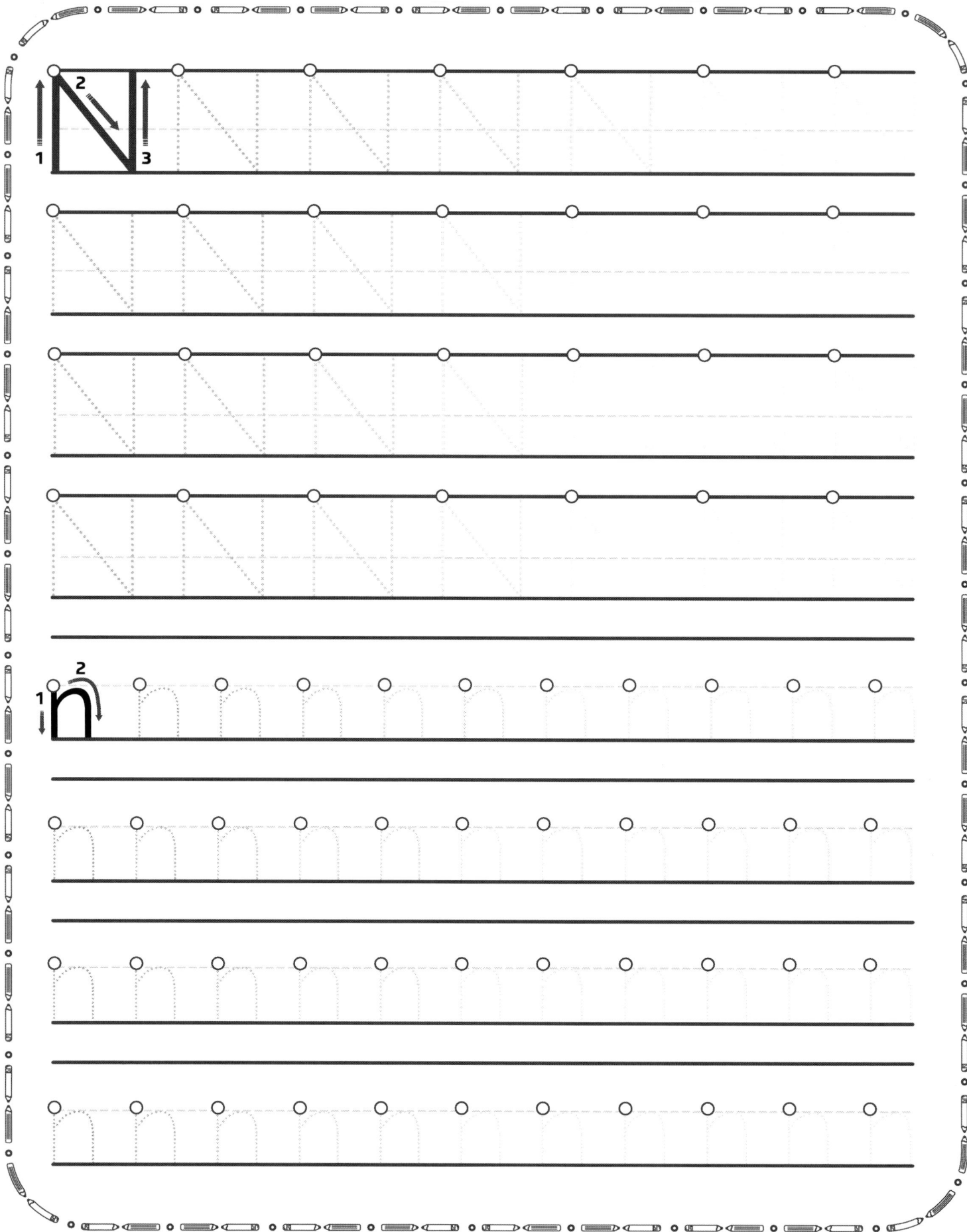

# NECKLACE

NECKLACE

NECKLACE

NECKLACE

## necklace

necklace

necklace

AaBbCcDdEeFfGgHhIiJjKkLlMm**Nn**OoPpQqRrSsTtUuVvWwXxYyZz

AaBbCcDdEeFfGgHhIiJjKkLlMmNn**Oo**PpQqRrSsTtUuVvWwXxYyZz

**1**

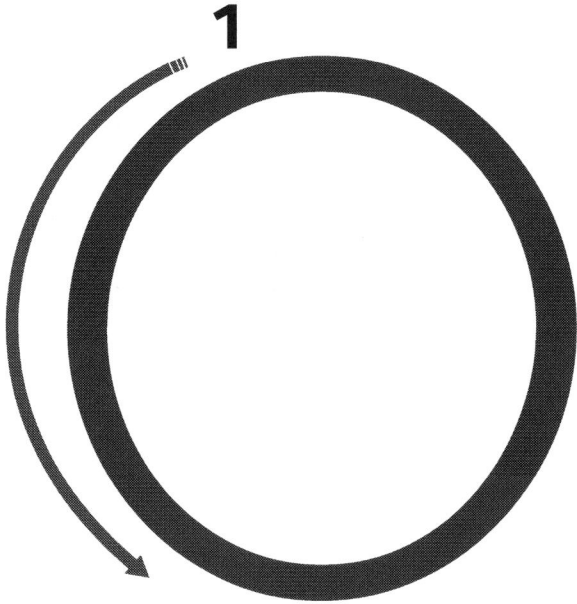

**1**

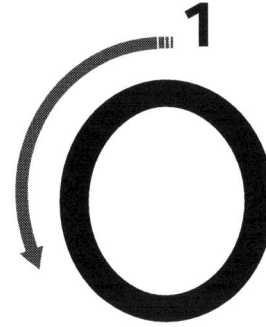

# Octopus

**1**

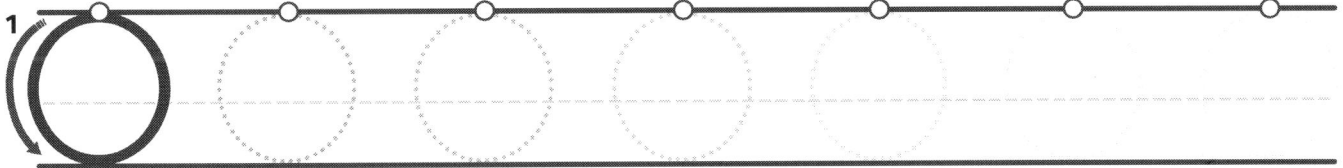

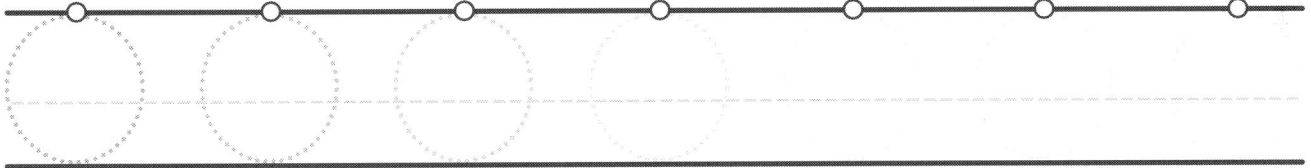

**1**

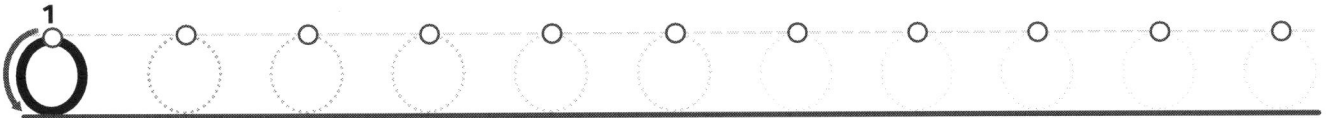

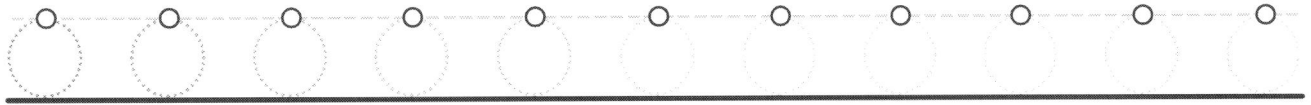

1

1

AaBbCcDdEeFfGgHhIiJjKkLlMmNn**Oo**PpQqRrSsTtUuVvWwXxYyZz

# OCTOPUS

OCTOPUS

OCTOPUS

OCTOPUS

## octopus octopus

octopus octopus

octopus octopus

octopus octopus

AaBbCcDdEeFfGgHhIiJjKkLlMmNn**Oo**PpQqRrSsTtUuVvWwXxYyZz

AaBbCcDdEeFfGgHhIiJjKkLlMmNnOo**Pp**QqRrSsTtUuVvWwXxYyZz

# Pig

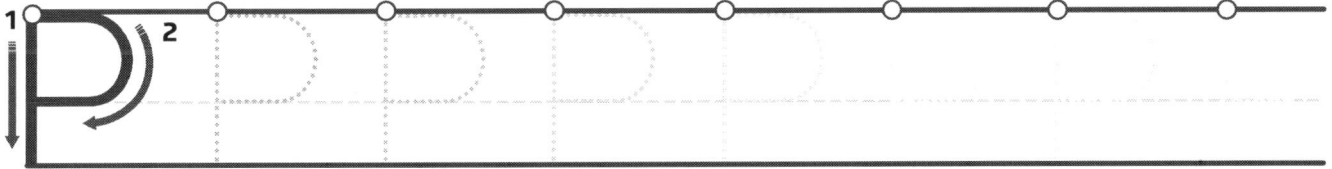

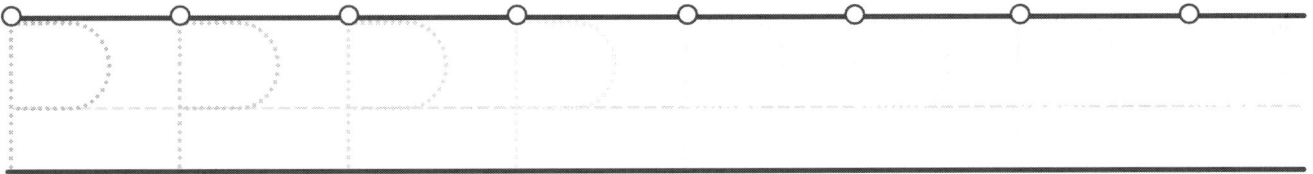

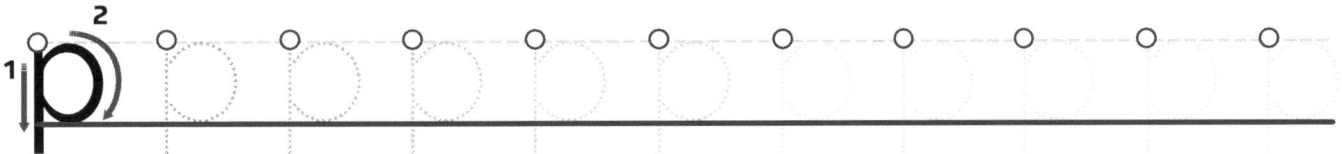

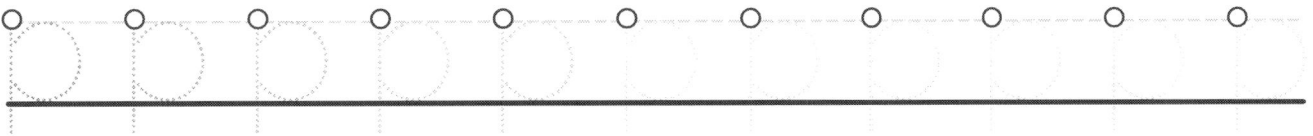

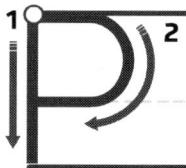
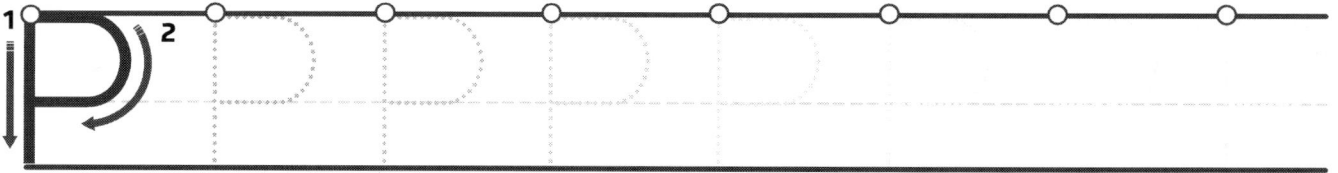
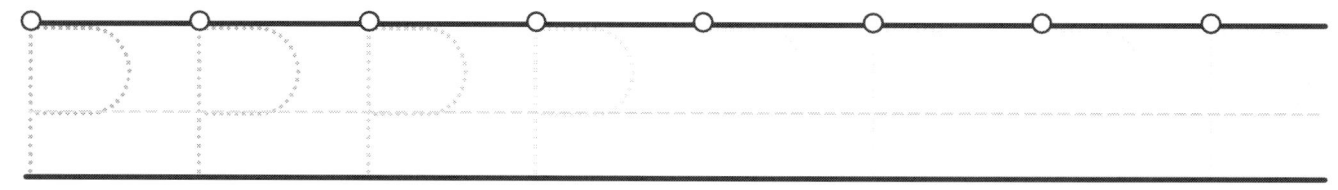
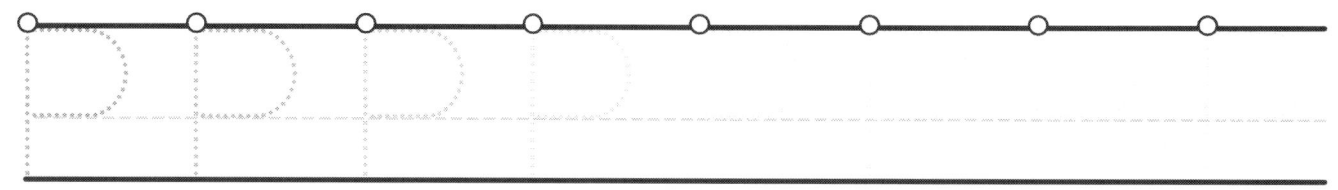
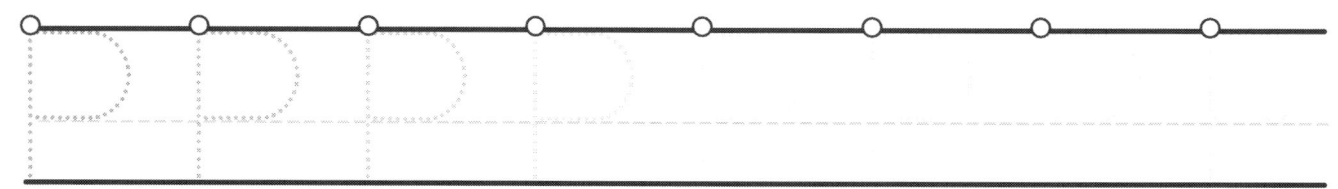
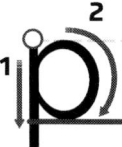
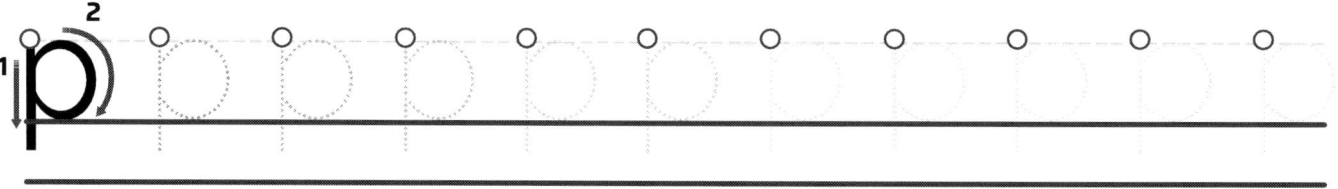
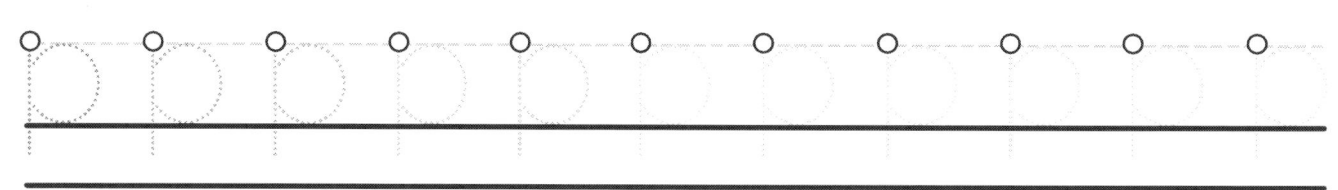
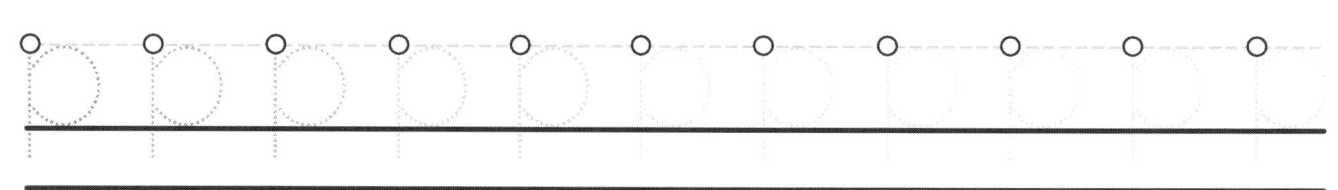
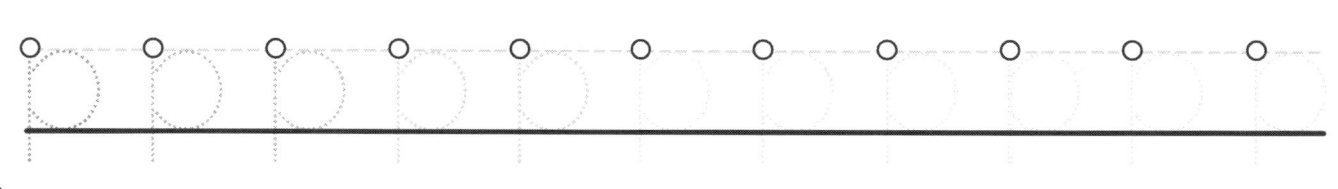

AaBbCcDdEeFfGgHhIiJjKkLlMmNnOo**Pp**QqRrSsTtUuVvWwXxYyZz

# PIG PIG PIG

PIG PIG PIG

PIG PIG PIG

PIG PIG PIG

## pig pig pig pig

pig pig pig pig

pig pig pig pig

pig pig pig pig

AaBbCcDdEeFfGgHhIiJjKkLlMmNnOo**Pp**QqRrSsTtUuVvWwXxYyZz

AaBbCcDdEeFfGgHhIiJjKkLlMmNnOoPpQqRrSsTtUuVvWwXxYyZz

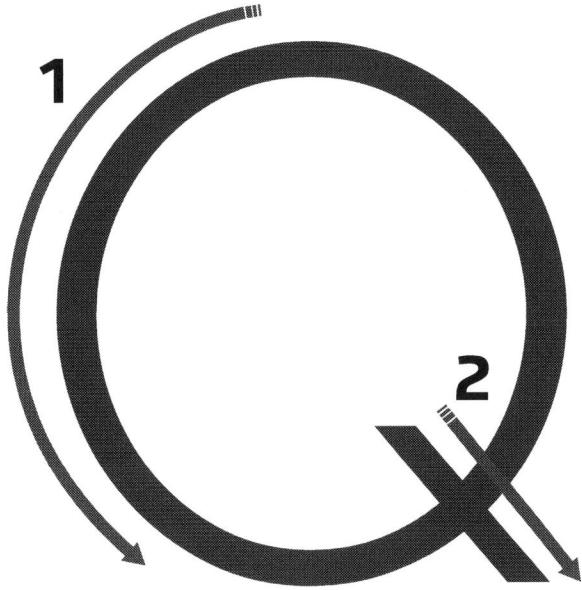
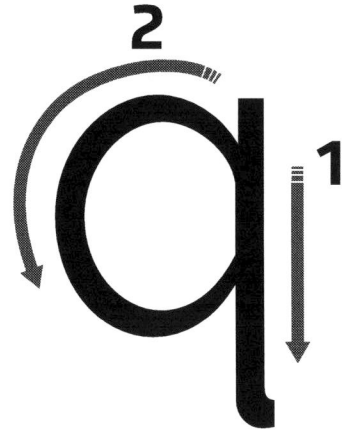

# Queen

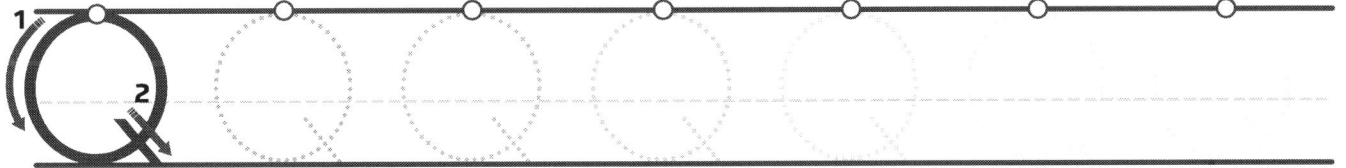
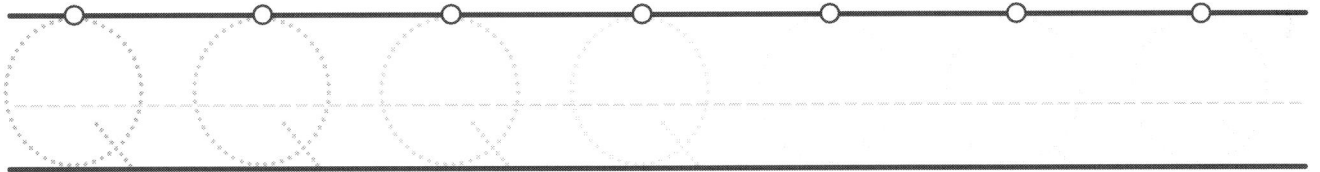
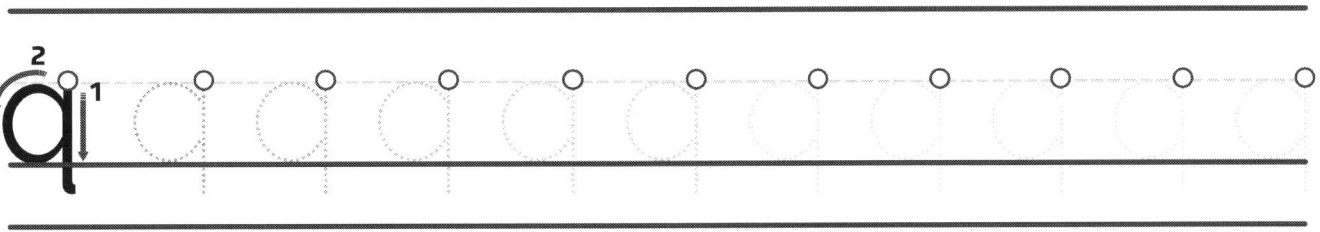
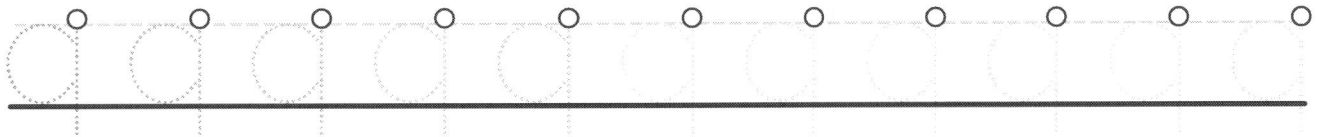

*AaBbCcDdEeFfGgHhIiJjKkLlMmNnOoPp**Qq**RrSsTtUuVvWwXxYyZz*

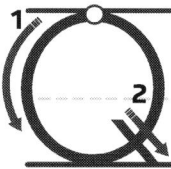

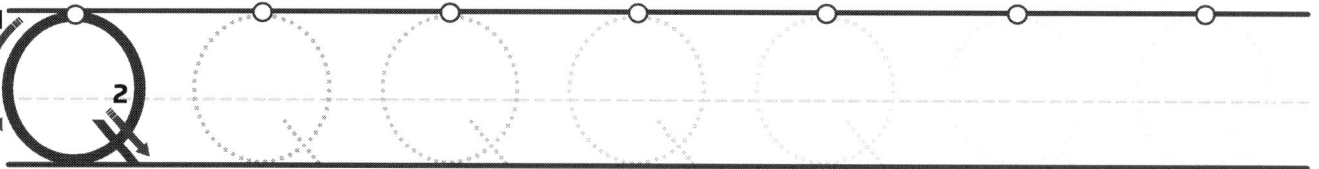

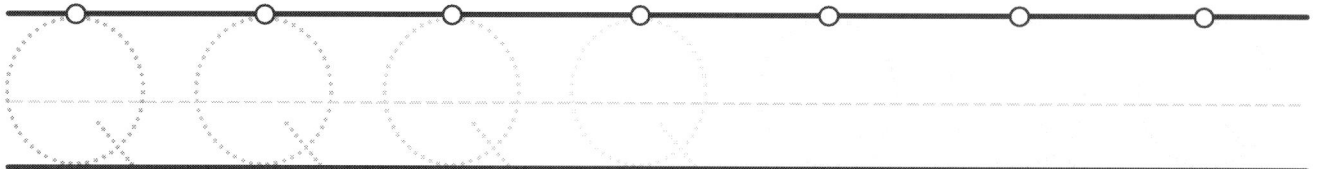

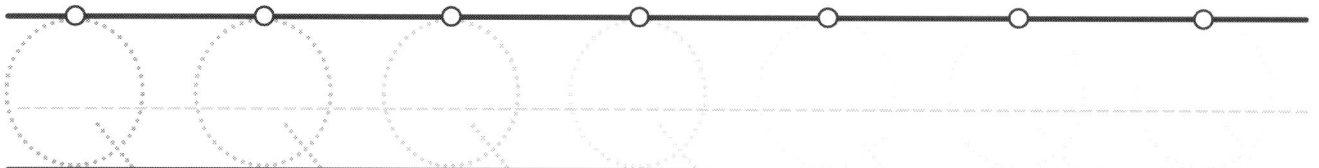

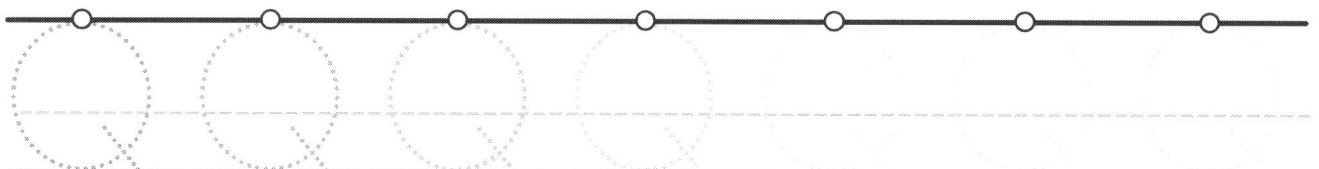

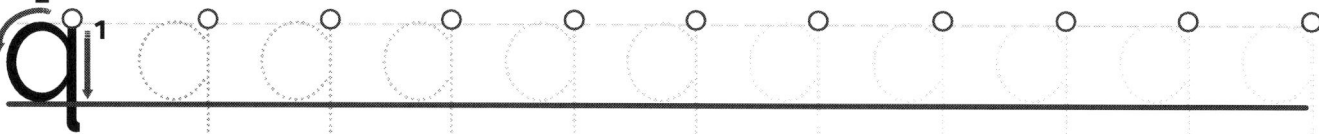

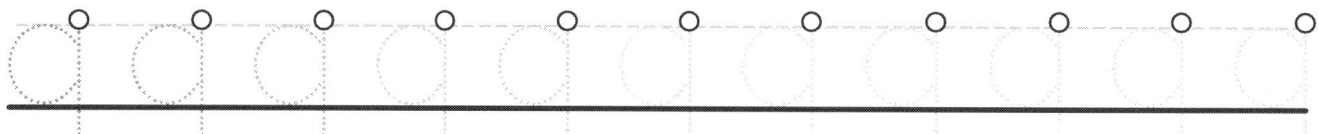

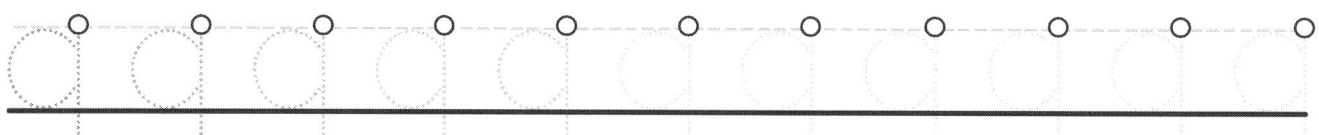

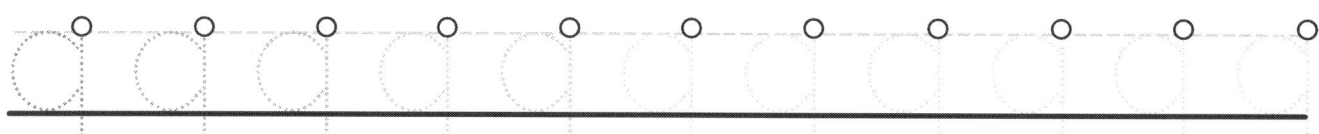

# QUEEN

QUEEN QUEEN

QUEEN QUEEN

QUEEN QUEEN

queen    queen

queen    queen

queen    queen

AaBbCcDdEeFfGgHhIiJjKkLlMmNnOoPp**Qq**RrSsTtUuVvWwXxYyZz

AaBbCcDdEeFfGgHhIiJjKkLlMmNnOoPpQq**Rr**SsTtUuVvWwXxYyZz

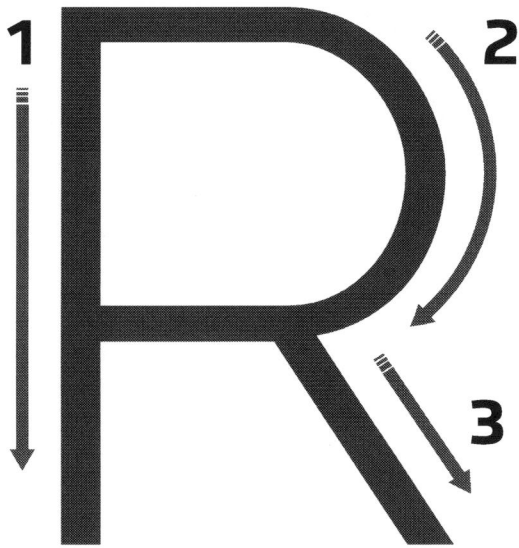

# Rabbit

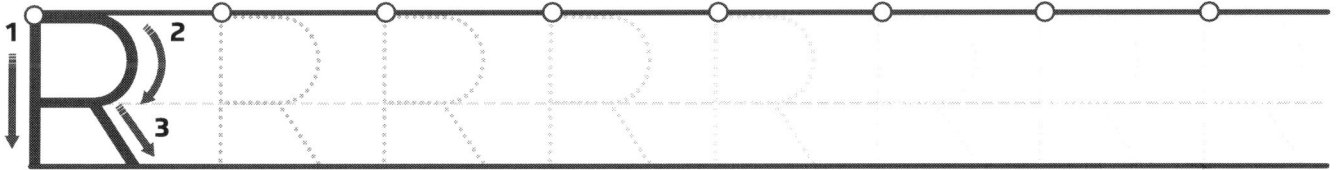
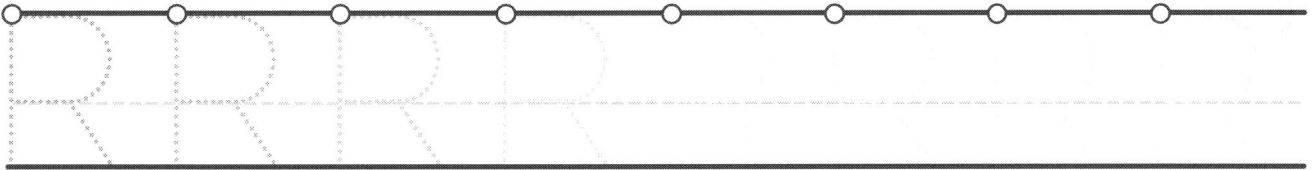
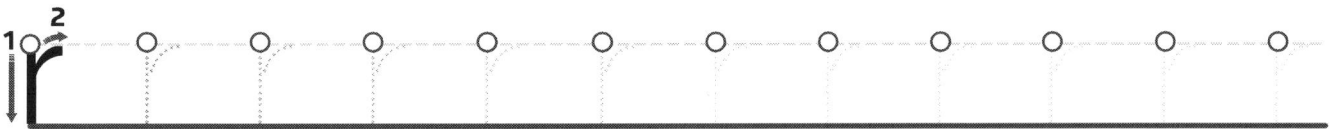
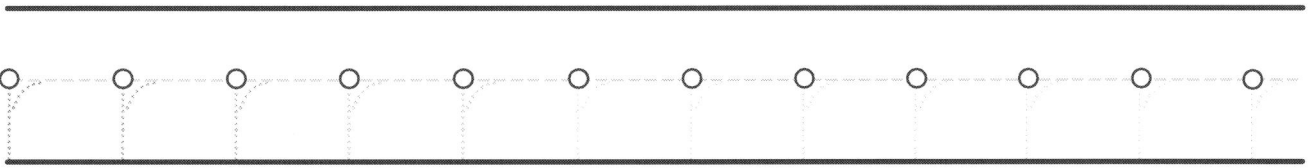

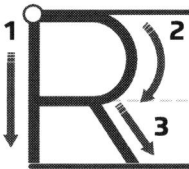
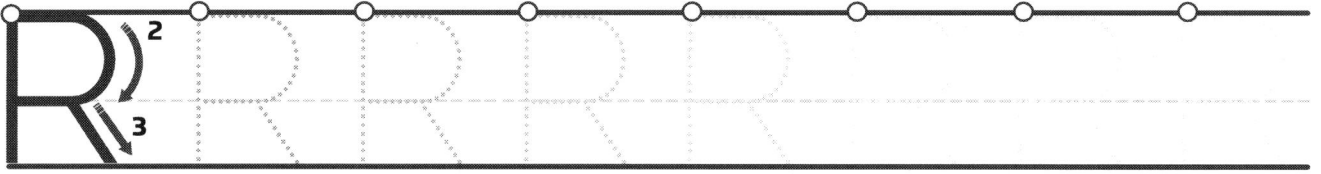
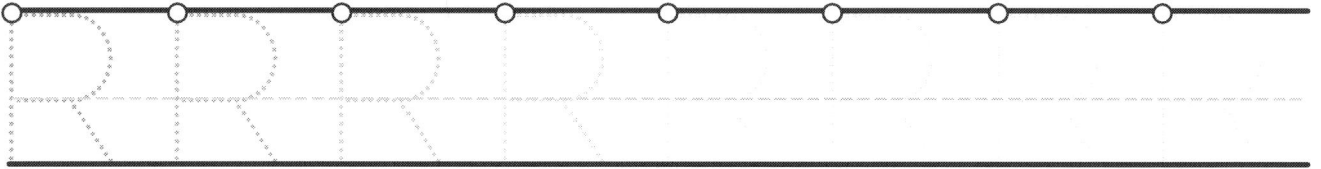
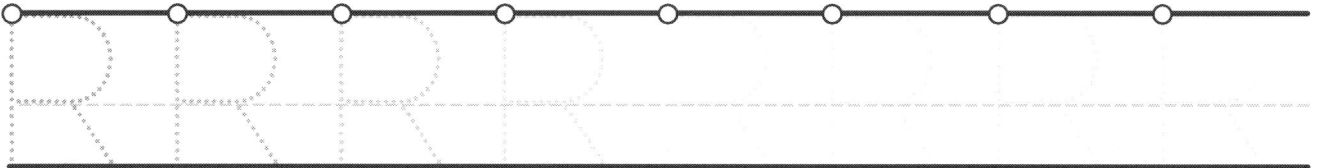
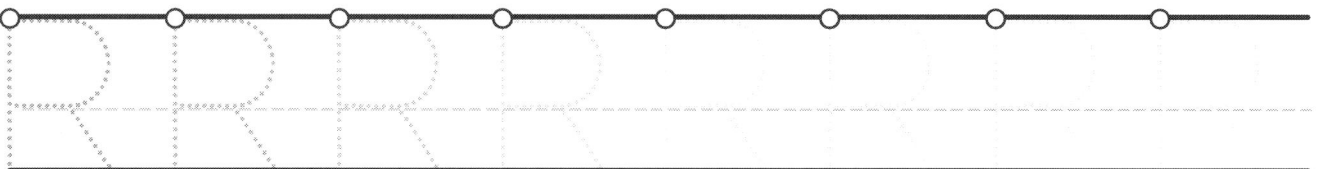

*AaBbCcDdEeFfGgHhIiJjKkLlMmNnOoPpQq**Rr**SsTtUuVvWwXxYyZz*

# RABBIT

RABBIT

RABBIT

RABBIT

## rabbit    rabbit

rabbit    rabbit

rabbit    rabbit

rabbit    rabbit

AaBbCcDdEeFfGgHhIiJjKkLlMmNnOoPpQq**Rr**SsTtUuVvWwXxYyZz

AaBbCcDdEeFfGgHhIiJjKkLlMmNnOoPpQqRrSsTtUuVvWwXxYyZz

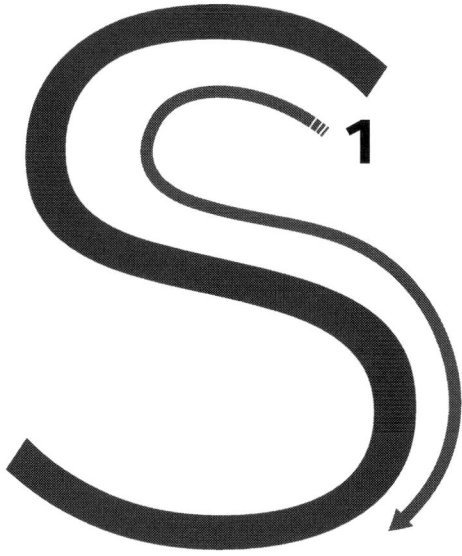

## Shark

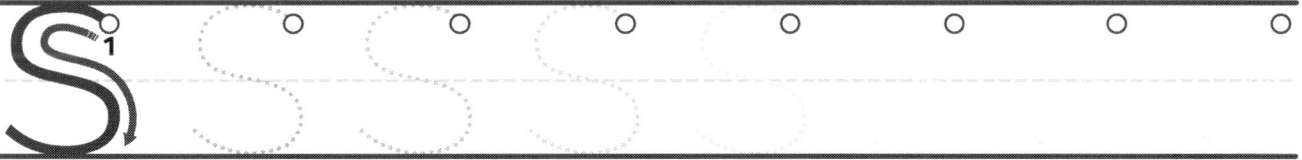

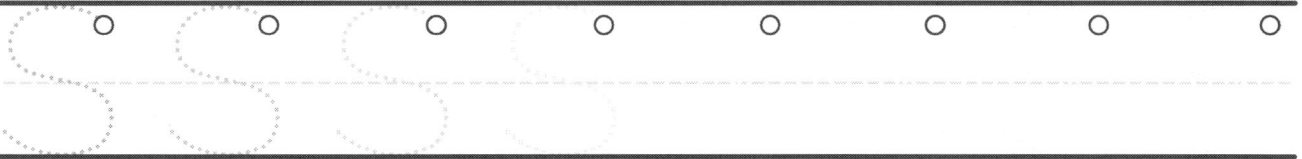

S S S S S S S S S

S S S S S S S S S

S S S S S S S S S

S S S S S S S S S

s s s s s s s s s s

s s s s s s s s s s

s s s s s s s s s s

s s s s s s s s s s

AaBbCcDdEeFfGgHhIiJjKkLlMmNnOoPpQqRr**Ss**TtUuVvWwXxYyZz

# SHARKSHARK

SHARKSHARK

SHARKSHARK

SHARKSHARK

## shark shark shark

shark shark shark

shark shark shark

AaBbCcDdEeFfGgHhIiJjKkLlMmNnOoPpQqRrSsTtUuVvWwXxYyZz

AaBbCcDdEeFfGgHhIiJjKkLlMmNnOoPpQqRrSsTtUuVvWwXxYyZz

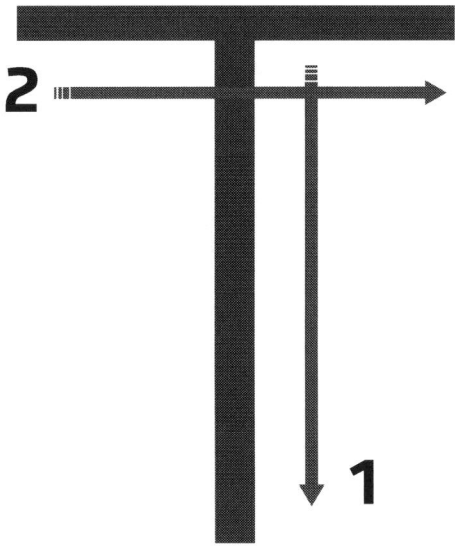

Tiger

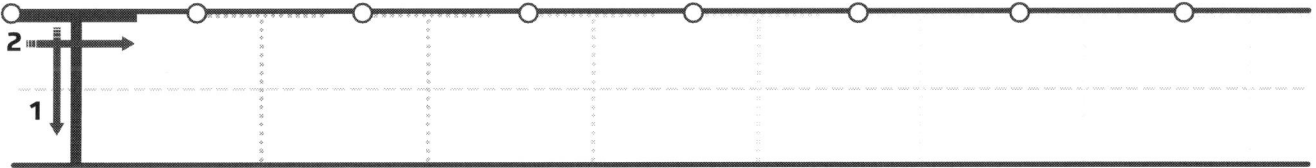

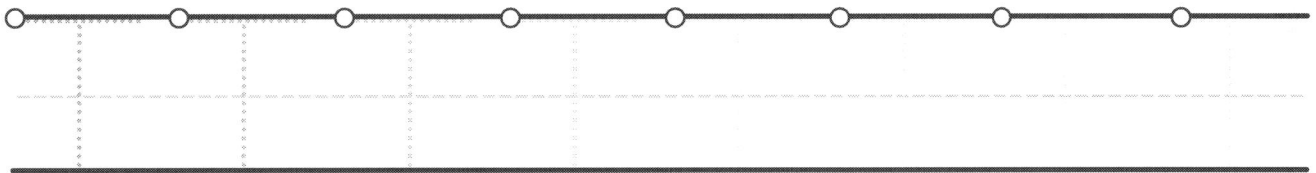

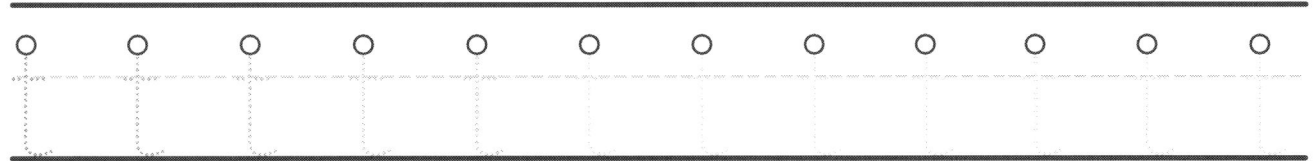

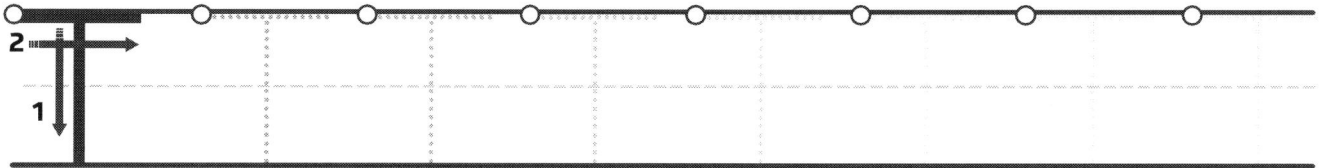

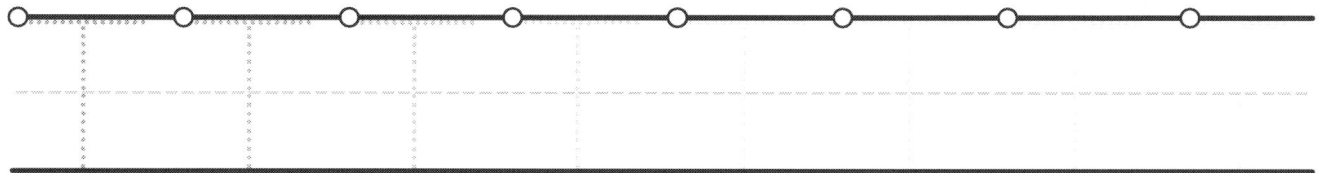

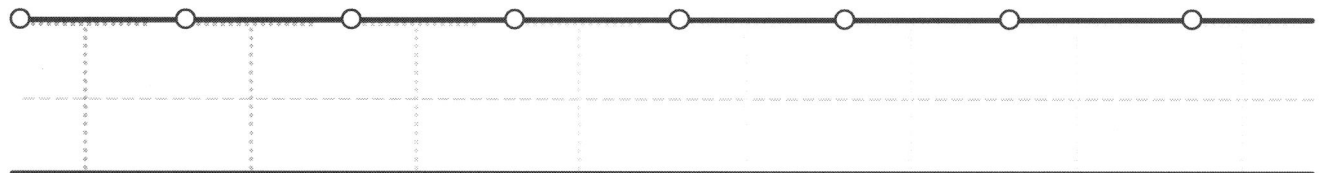

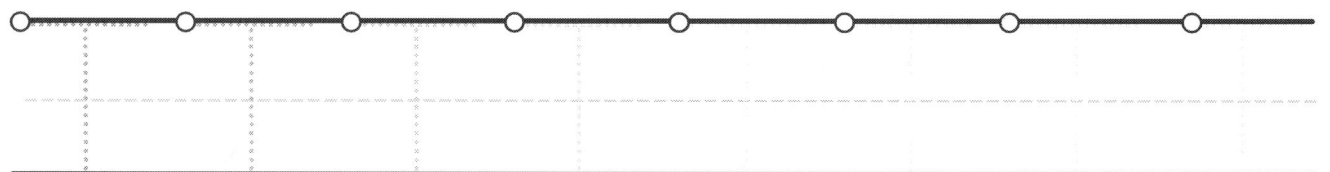

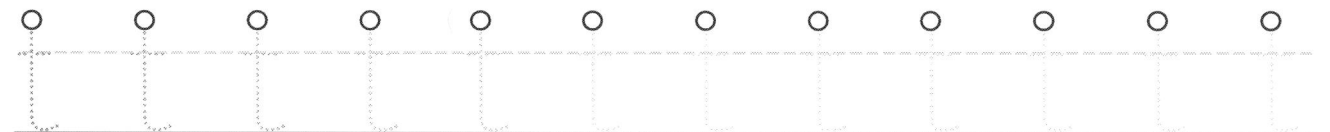

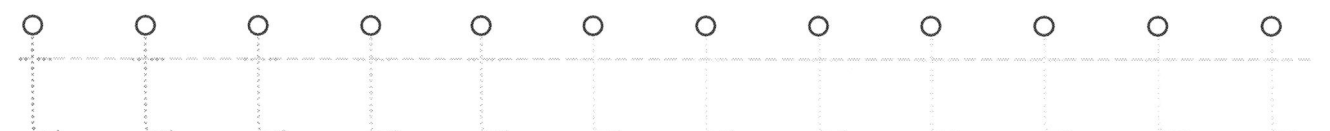

# TIGER TIGER

TIGER TIGER

TIGER TIGER

TIGER TIGER

## tiger tiger tiger

tiger tiger tiger

tiger tiger tiger

AaBbCcDdEeFfGgHhIiJjKkLlMmNnOoPpQqRrSsTt**Uu**VvWwXxYyZz

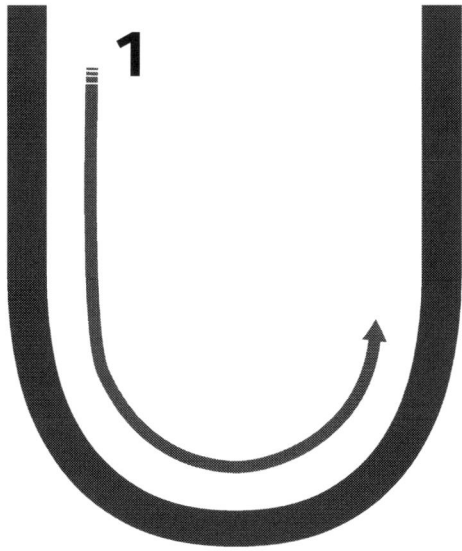

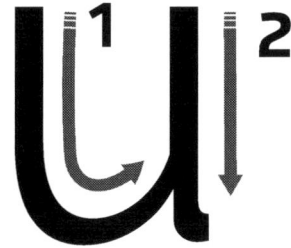

# Umbrella

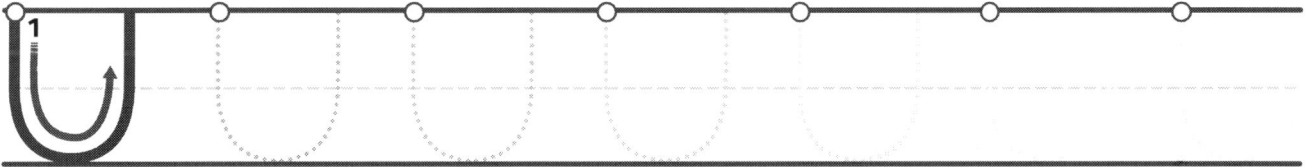

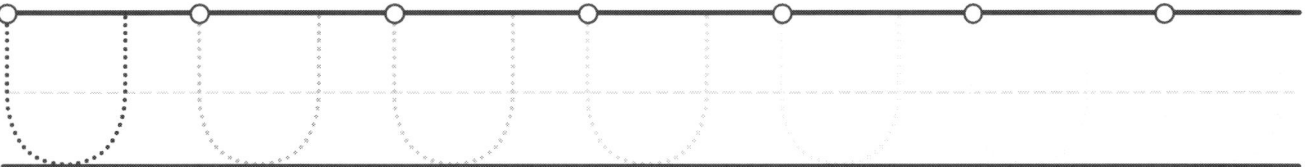

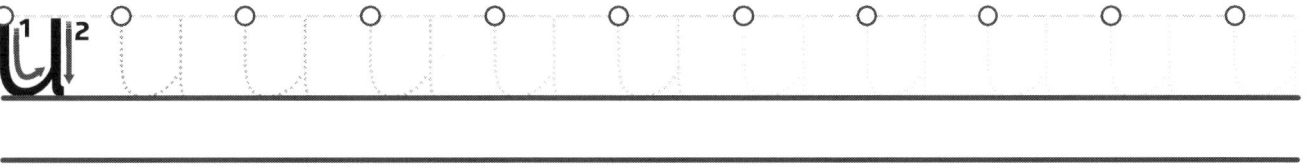

AaBbCcDdEeFfGgHhIiJjKkLlMmNnOoPpQqRrSsTt**Uu**VvWwXxYyZz

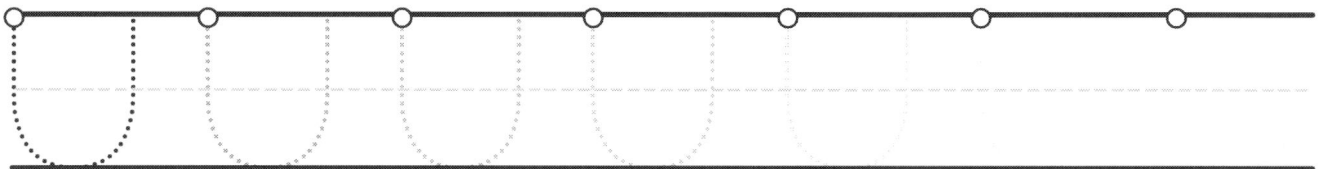

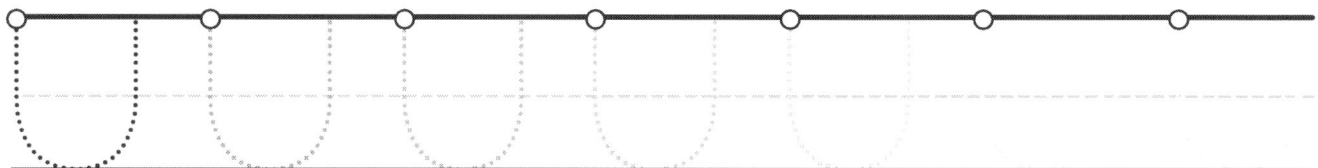

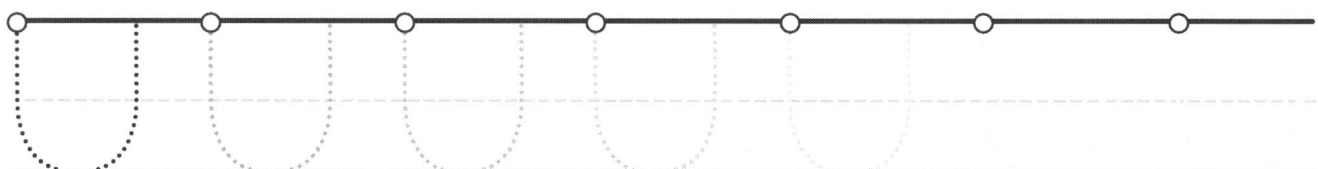

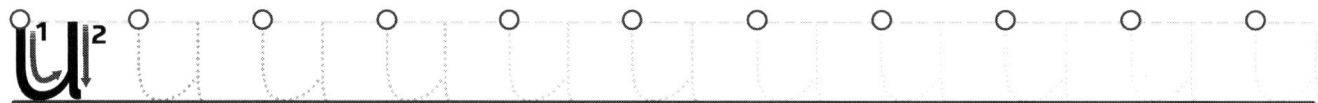

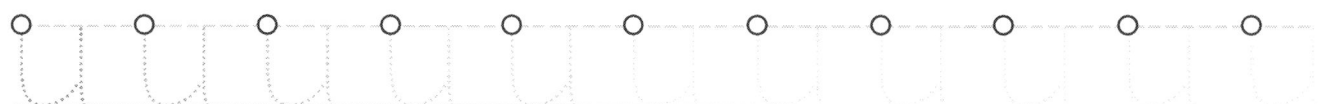

# UMBRELLA

UMBRELLA

UMBRELLA

UMBRELLA

# umbrella umbrella

umbrella umbrella

umbrella umbrella

umbrella umbrella

AaBbCcDdEeFfGgHhIiJjKkLlMmNnOoPpQqRrSsTt**UuVvWwXxYyZz**

AaBbCcDdEeFfGgHhIiJjKkLlMmNnOoPpQqRrSsTtUu**Vv**WwXxYyZz

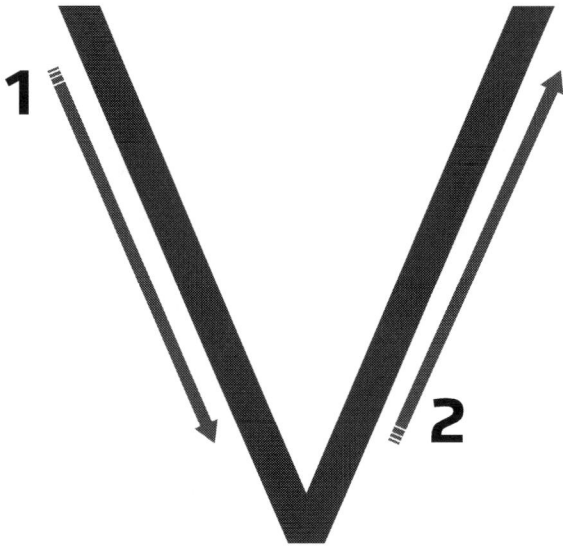

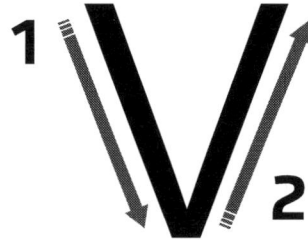

# Vehicle

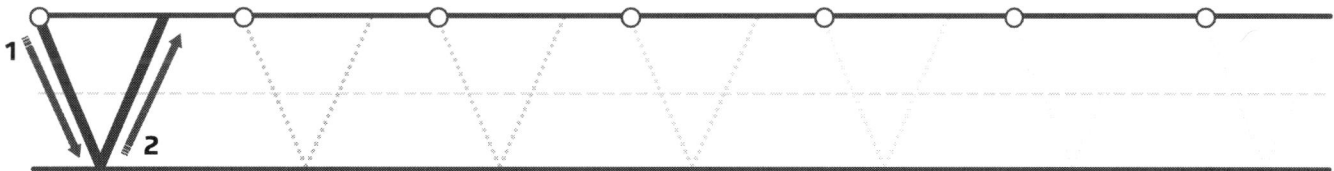

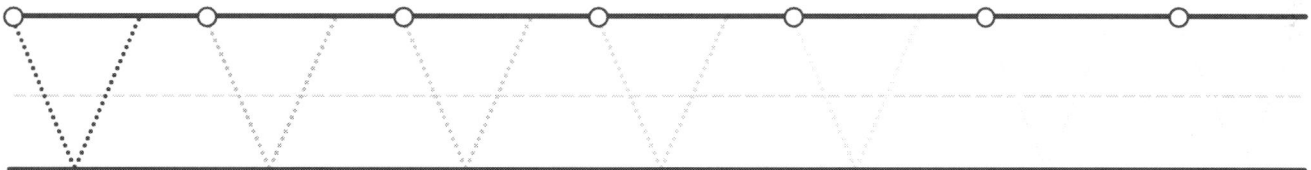

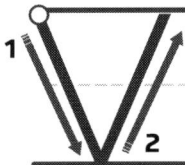

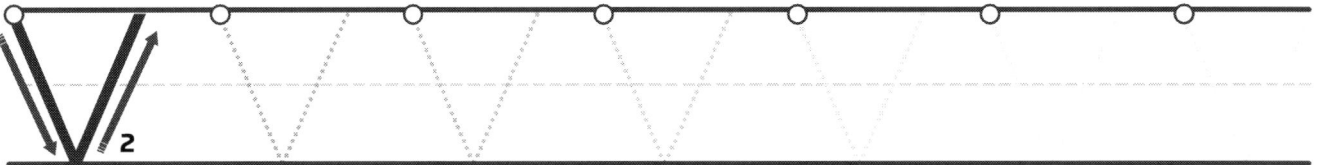

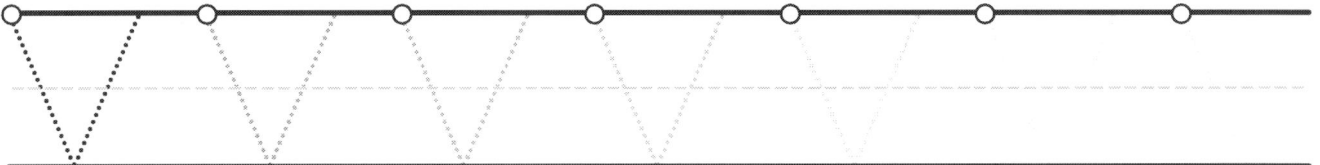

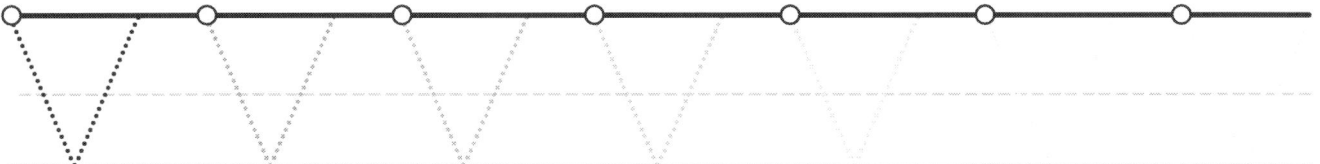

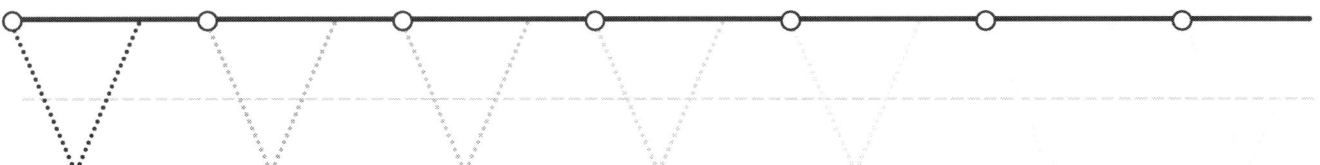

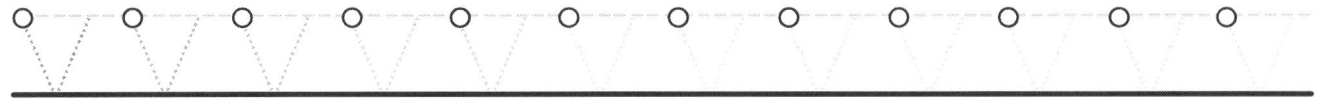

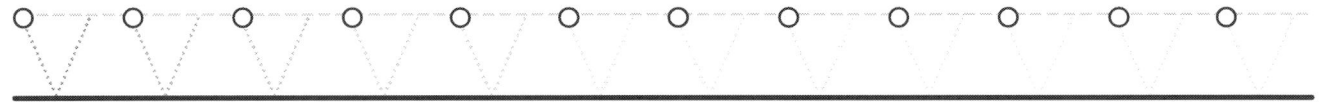

AaBbCcDdEeFfGgHhIiJjKkLlMmNnOoPpQqRrSsTtUu**Vv**WwXxYyZz

# VEHICLE

VEHICLE

VEHICLE

VEHICLE

## vehicle vehicle

vehicle vehicle

vehicle vehicle

vehicle vehicle

AaBbCcDdEeFfGgHhIiJjKkLlMmNnOoPpQqRrSsTtUu**Vv**WwXxYyZz

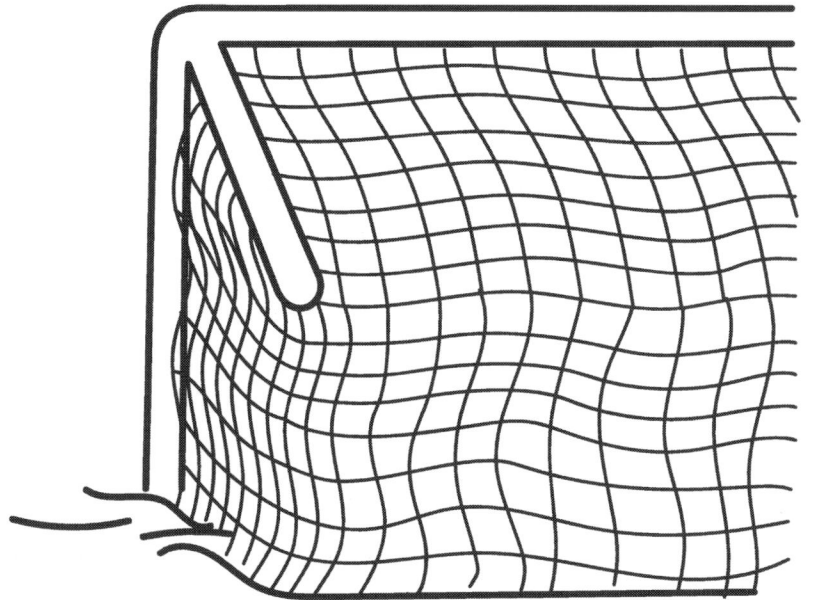

AaBbCcDdEeFfGgHhIiJjKkLlMmNnOoPpQqRrSsTtUuVv**Ww**XxYyZz

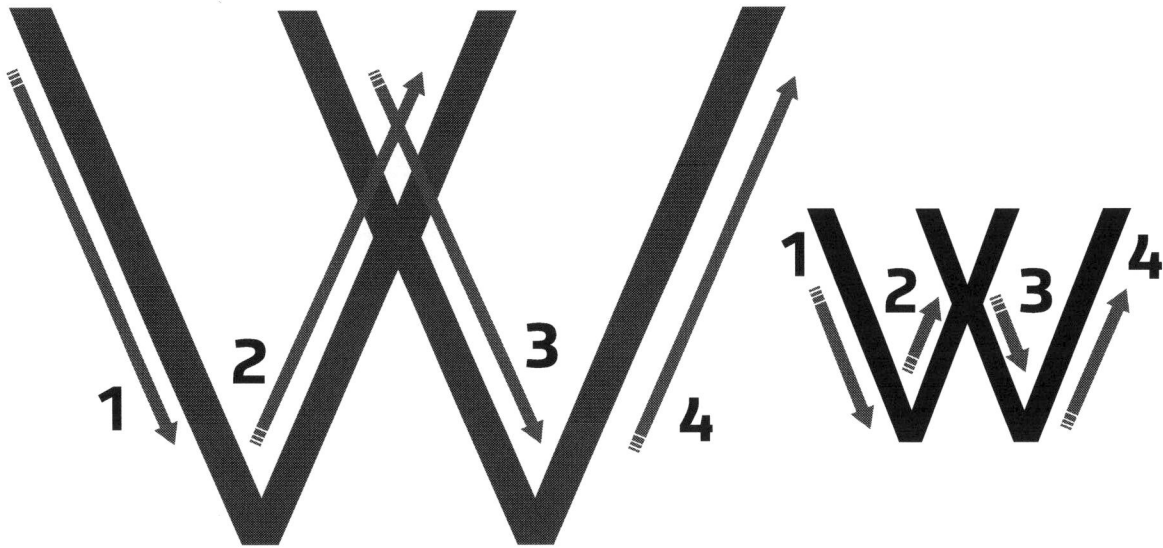

# Waterpolo

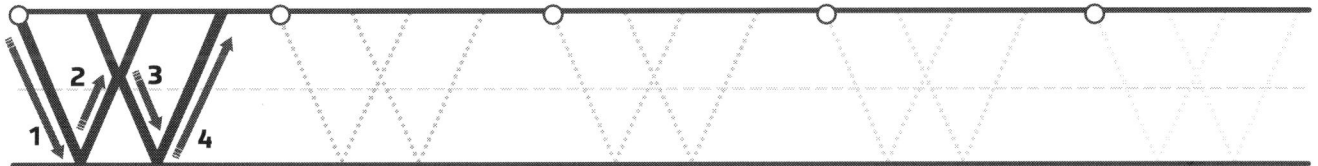

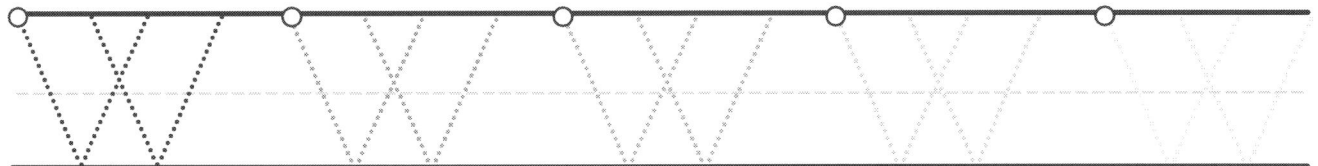

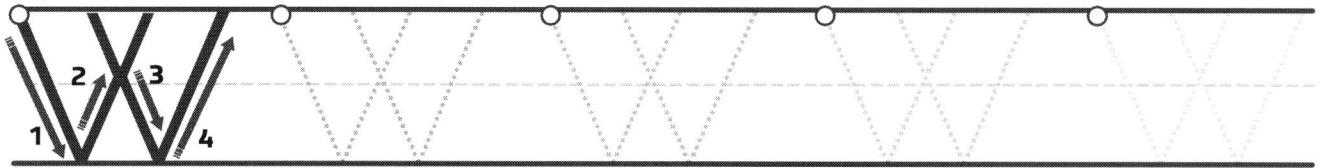

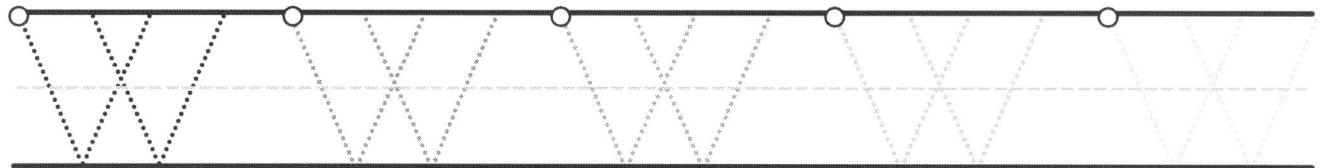

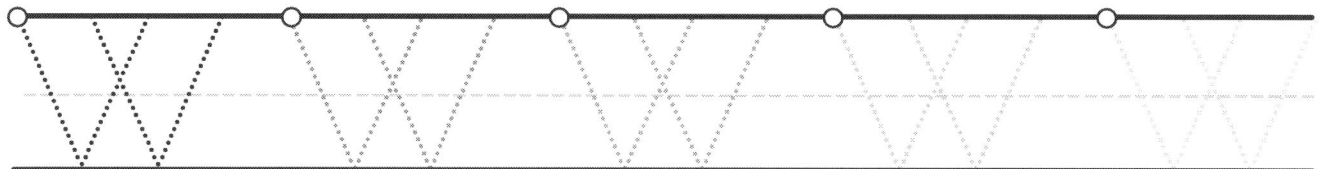

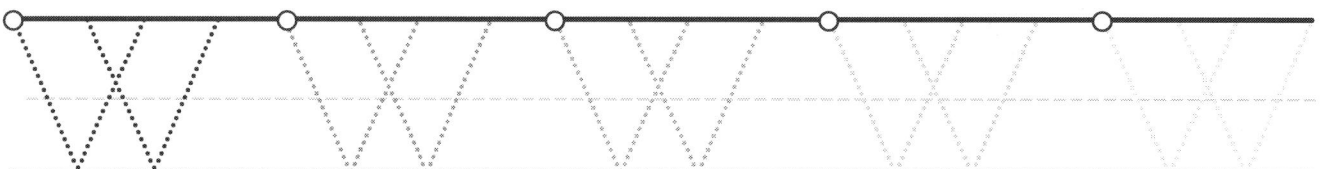

# WATERPOLO

WATERPOLO

WATERPOLO

WATERPOLO

## waterpolo

waterpolo

waterpolo

waterpolo

AaBbCcDdEeFfGgHhIiJjKkLlMmNnOoPpQqRrSsTtUuVv**Ww**XxYyZz

AaBbCcDdEeFfGgHhIiJjKkLlMmNnOoPpQqRrSsTtUuVvWwXxYyZz

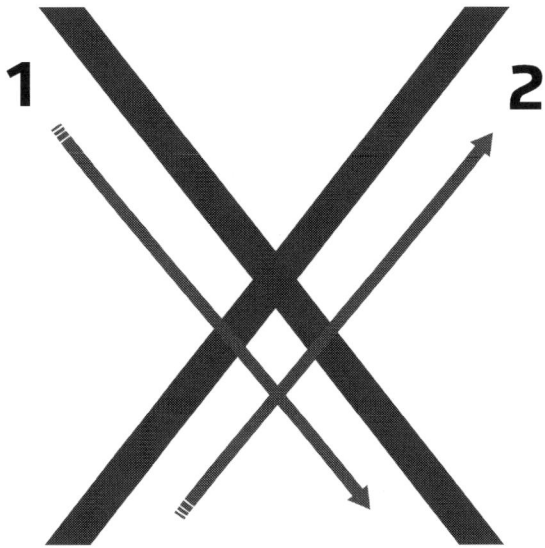

# Xylophone

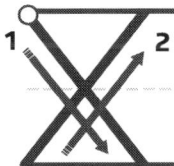

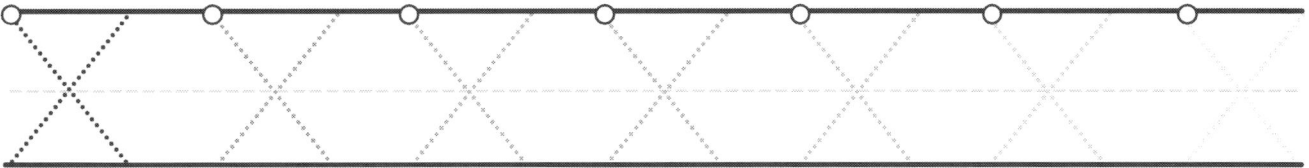

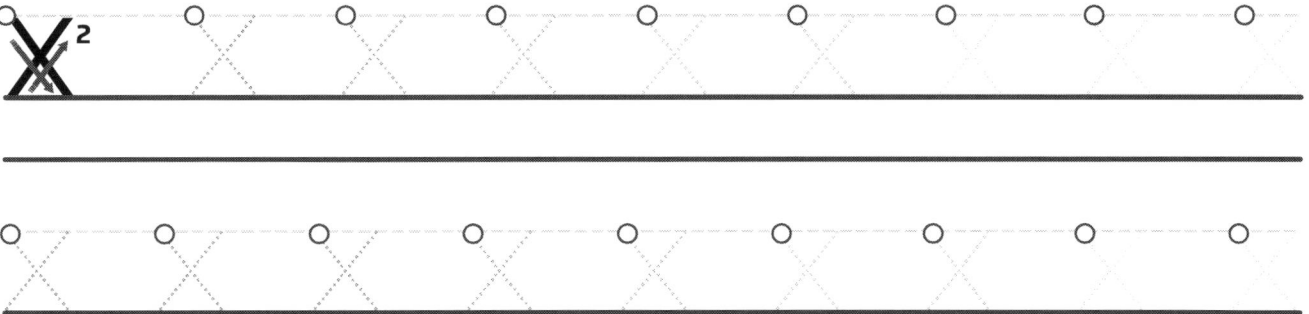

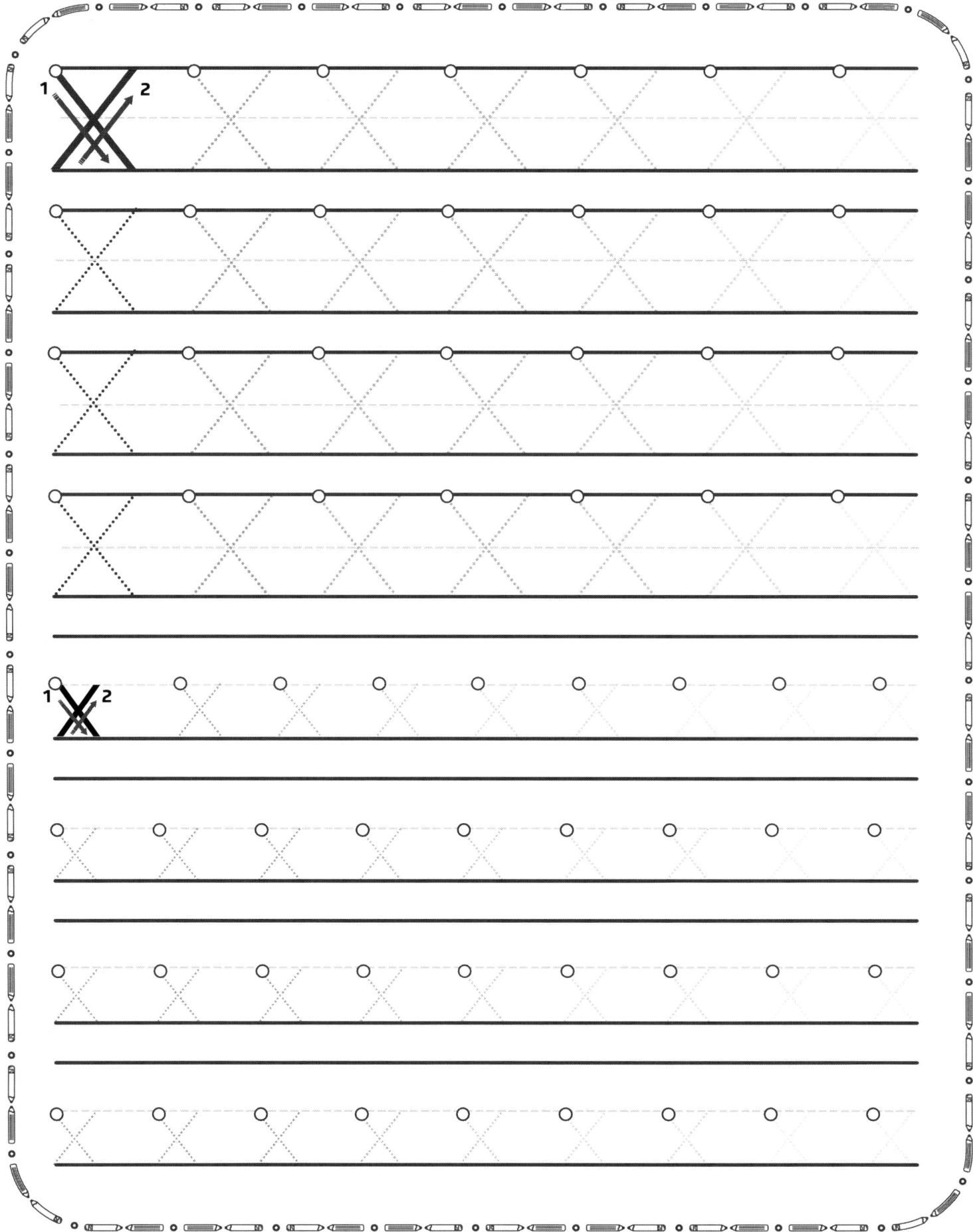

# XYLOPHONE

XYLOPHONE

XYLOPHONE

XYLOPHONE

## xylophone

xylophone

xylophone

xylophone

AaBbCcDdEeFfGgHhIiJjKkLlMmNnOoPpQqRrSsTtUuVvWwXxYyZz

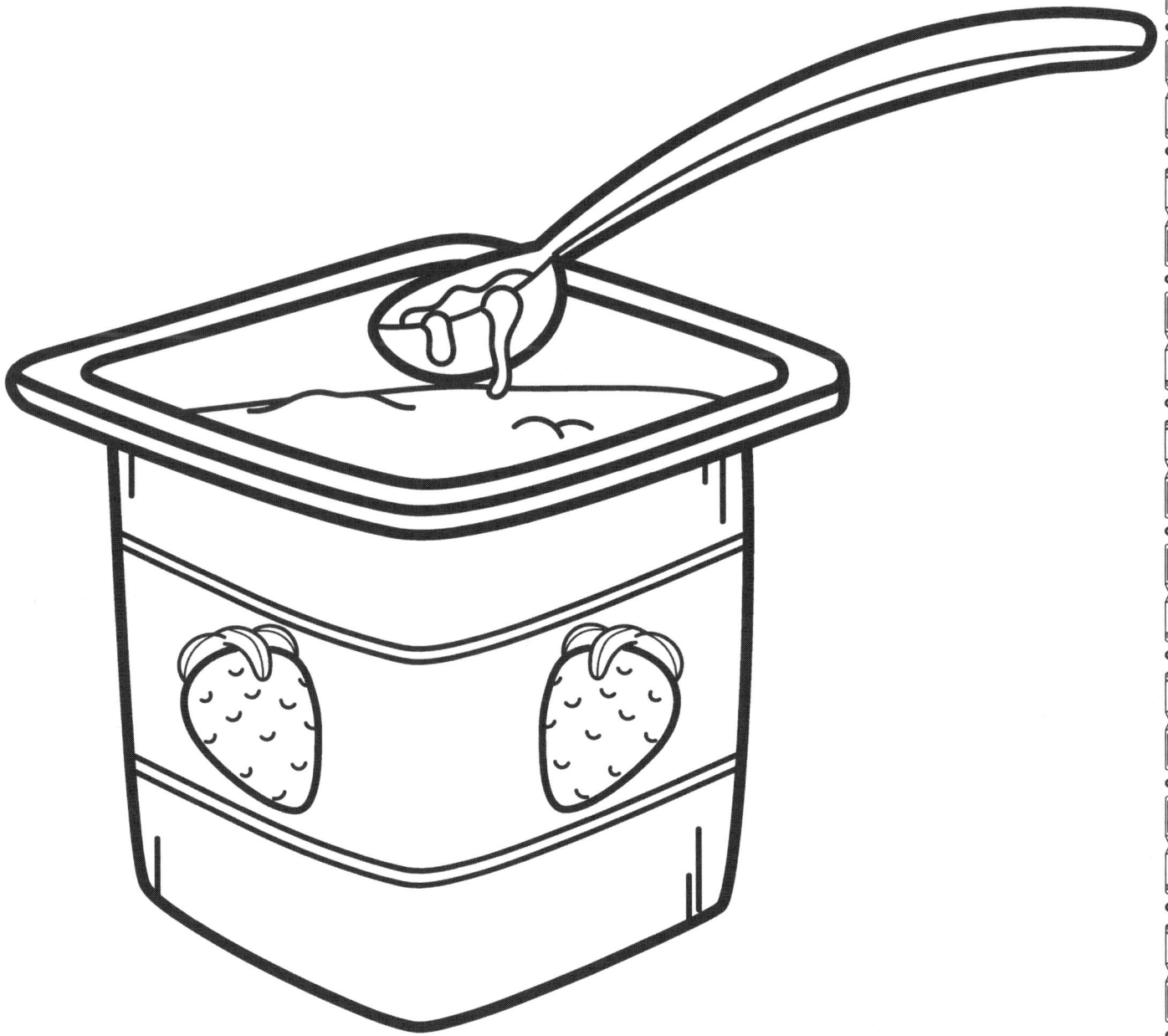

AaBbCcDdEeFfGgHhIiJjKkLlMmNnOoPpQqRrSsTtUuVvWwXxYyZz

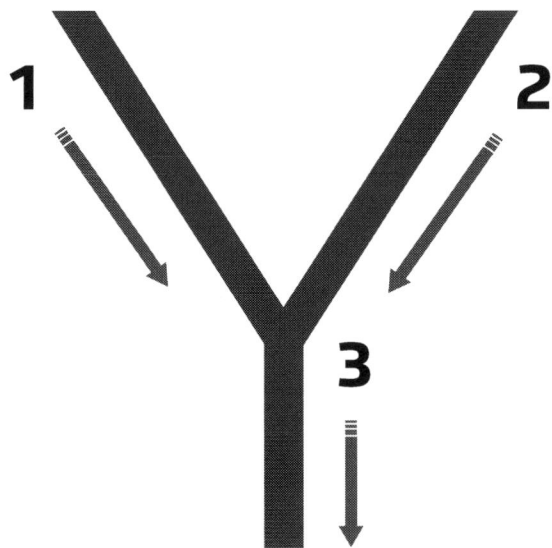
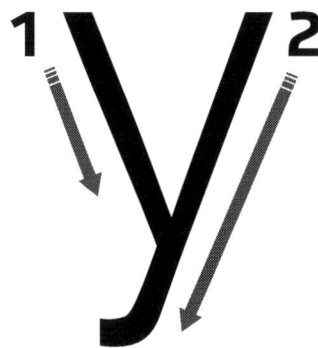

# Yogurt

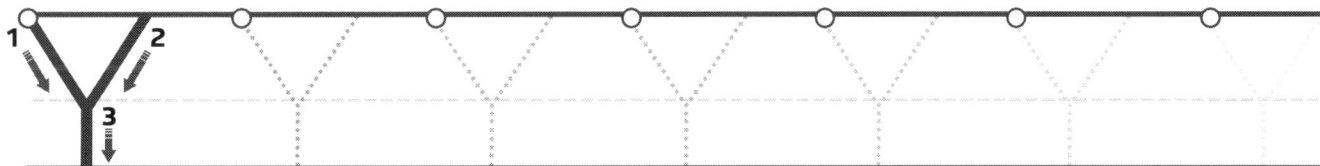
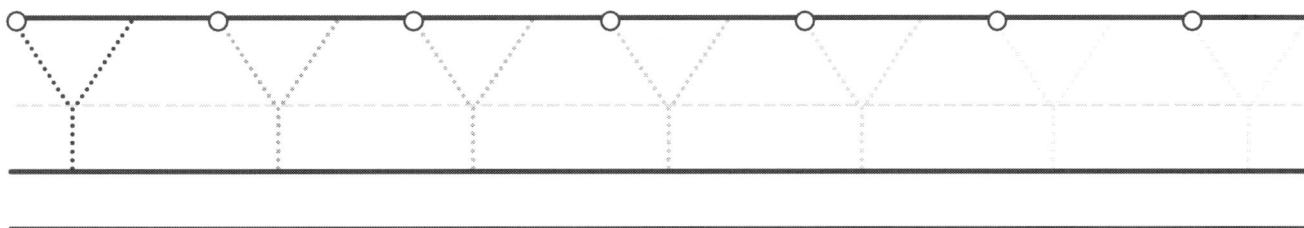
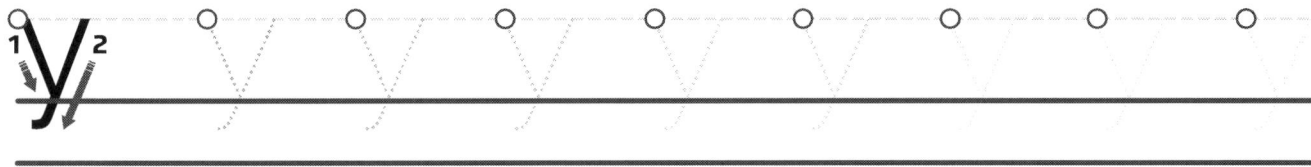
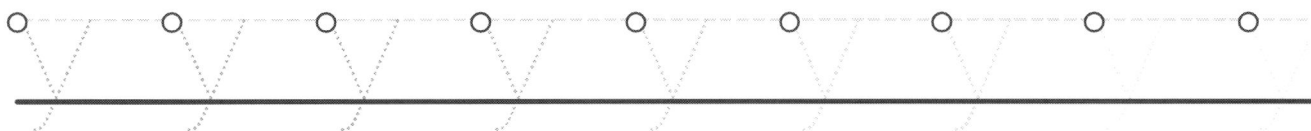

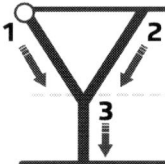

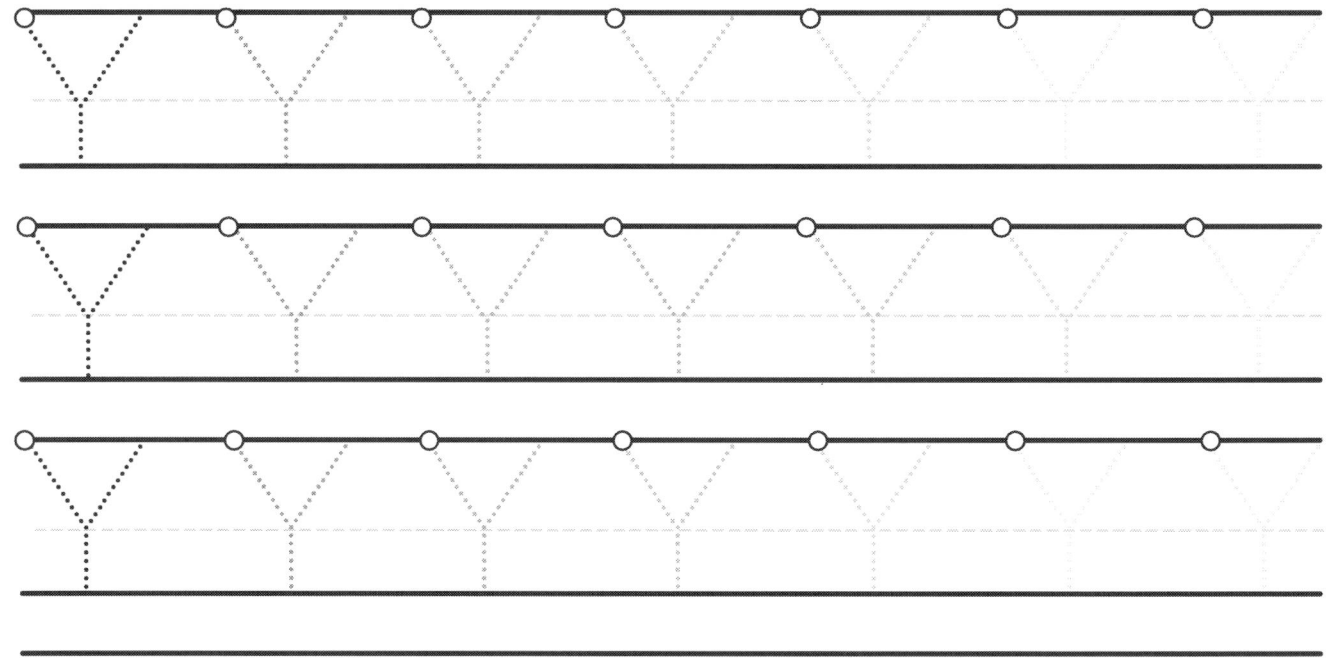

# YOGURT

YOGURT

YOGURT

YOGURT

## yogurt     yogurt

yogurt     yogurt

yogurt     yogurt

yogurt     yogurt

AaBbCcDdEeFfGgHhIiJjKkLlMmNnOoPpQqRrSsTtUuVvWwXxYyZz

AaBbCcDdEeFfGgHhIiJjKkLlMmNnOoPpQqRrSsTtUuVvWwXxYyZz

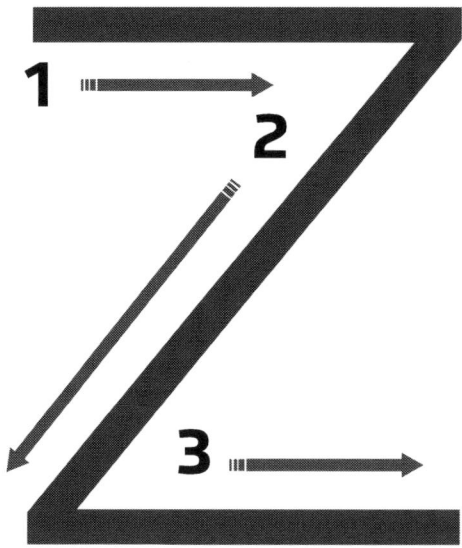
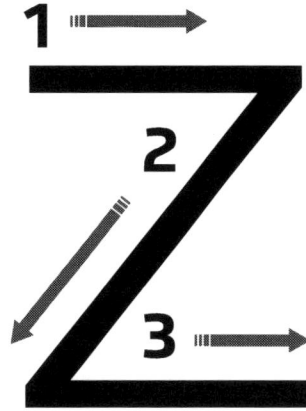

# zebra

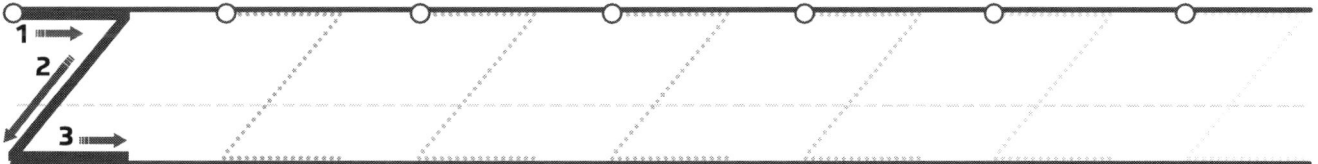
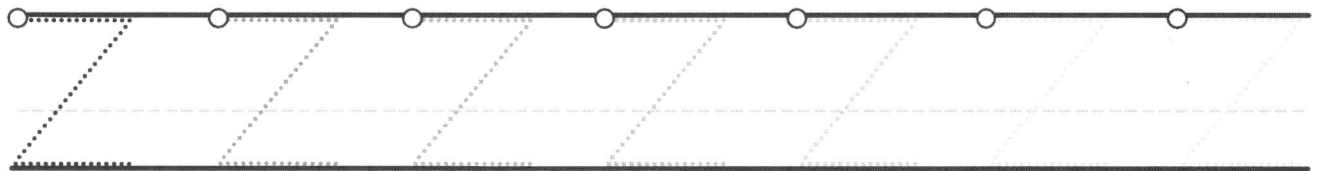
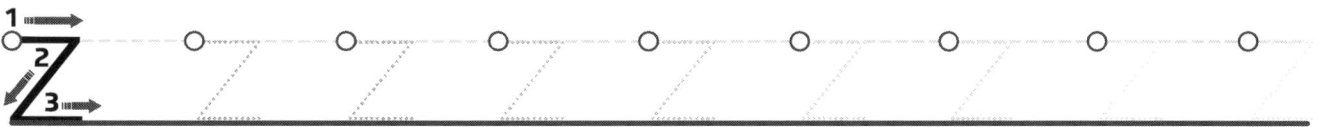

*AaBbCcDdEeFfGgHhIiJjKkLlMmNnOoPpQqRrSsTtUuVvWwXxYy**Zz***

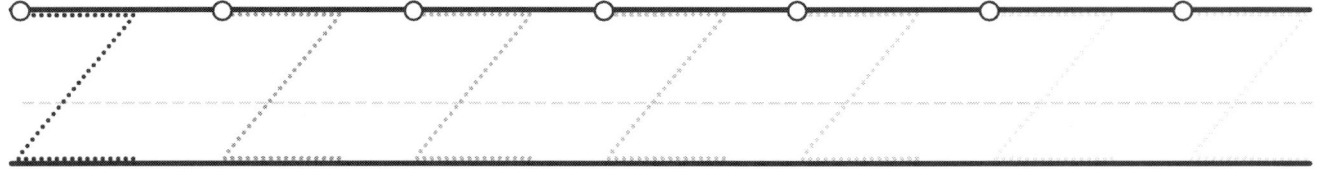

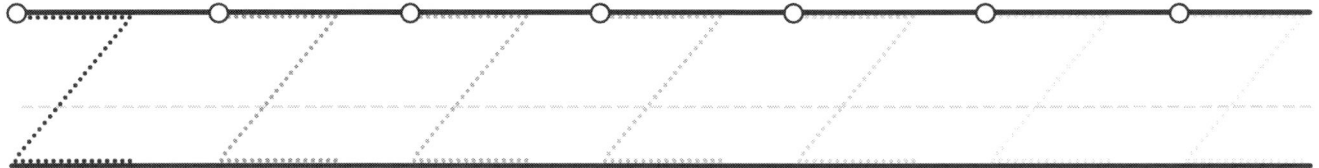

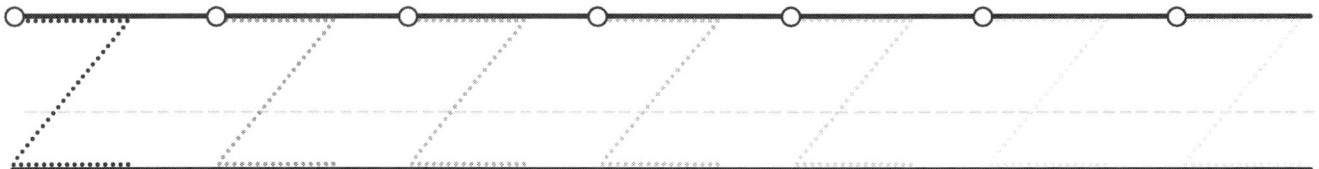

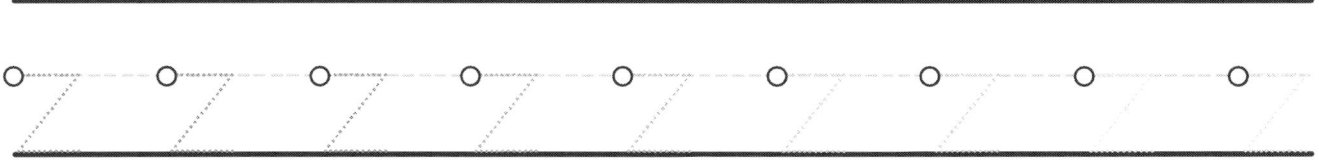

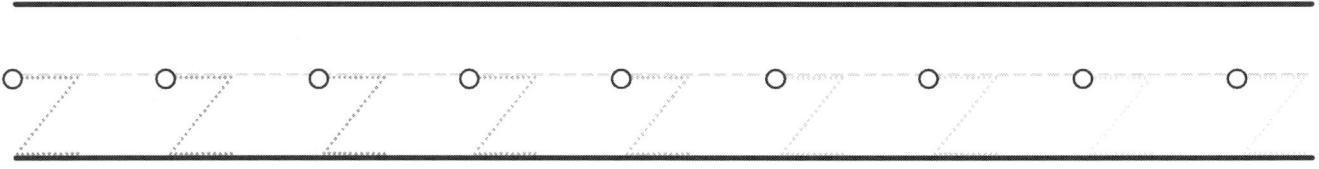

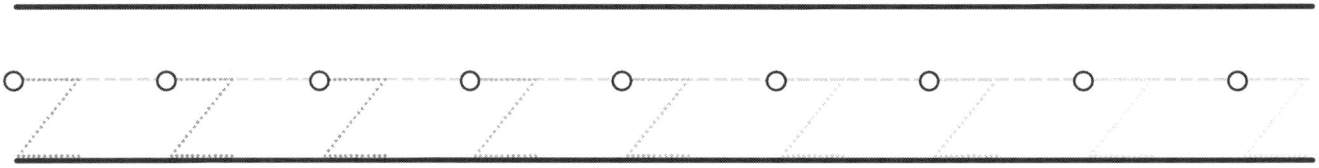

# ZEBRA ZEBRA

ZEBRA ZEBRA

ZEBRA ZEBRA

ZEBRA ZEBRA

zebra zebra

zebra zebra

zebra zebra

zebra zebra

AaBbCcDdEeFfGgHhIiJjKkLlMmNnOoPpQqRrSsTtUuVvWwXxYyZz

If you have any questions, comments or suggestions, feel free to contact us:

jadier.illustrations@gmail.com

You can also follow us on IG:

# @jadierillustrations

I would really appreciate it if you could take a few minutes of your time and leave your review on Amazon, as a independent author those reviews mean a lot to us.

Thank you very much and I hope you have enjoyed and learned a lot!